A HISTORY
of
IZARD COUNTY
ARKANSAS

KARR SHANNON, A.B., LL.B.
Columnist and Feature Writer for Arkansas Democrat
Little Rock, Arkansas

Published By
DEMOCRAT PRINTING AND LITHOGRAPHING CO.
Little Rock, Arkansas

Notice

In many older books, foxing (or discoloration) occurs and, in some instances, print lightens with wear and age. Reprinted books, such as this, often duplicate these flaws, notwithstanding efforts to reduce or eliminate them. The pages of this reprint have been digitally enhanced and, where possible, the flaws eliminated in order to provide clarity of content and a pleasant reading experience.

A History of Izard County, Arkansas

Copyright © 1947, Karr Shannon

Originally published
Little Rock, Arkansas
1947

Reprinted by:

Janaway Publishing, Inc.
732 Kelsey Ct.
Santa Maria, California 93454
(805) 925-1038
www.janawaygenealogy.com

2012

ISBN: 978-1-59641-281-1

Made in the United States of America

INTRODUCTION

THIS VOLUME is an attempt to describe in brief the main facts of the history of our county. I confess, before my critics accuse, that many facts and figures have been omitted as unnecessary to the story of Izard County, or because they could not be ascertained. This book is devoted chiefly to the people who fashioned and builded a county and helped it to progress, and the selection of characters and events has not been without care and painstaking.

The compilation is the outgrowth of pretentious historic study—months of grubbing in old newspapers, old letters, old legal documents, old records and books. It is the result of original research and personal contact with reliable characters who have freely contributed to the work. It has required many interviews and a vast amount of correspondence.

Much of the material has been chronicled as result of conversations years ago with some of our fine old citizens who have passed on—Dr. E. A. Baxter, Tom Watkins, T. H. Linn, John H. Woods, Capt. F. M. Hanley, J. W. C. Gardner, M. E. Clark and Judge John C. Ashley.

In addition to these, I am deeply indebted to Hon. Wilbur D. Mills, Member of Congress, who was instrumental in getting much information about the various post offices from the Post Office Department and the National Archives; to C. G. Hall, Secretary of State, for the use of his records relative to county officials; to the State Banking Department for information about the county's banks; to Dallas T. Herndon, State Historian, for use of his library; to the Izard County newspaper editors, C. L. Coger and Neill Brooks, for the use of their files and other aids; to the Izard County officials, and Postmaster R. O. Tomlinson of Melbourne, who responded most graciously to all requests, and to De E. Bradshaw, John Q. Wolf, P. A. Billingsley, Mrs. Pearl Dixon and many others.

I am also indebted to Karr Shannon, Jr., for helping me assemble the material and for typing the final manuscript.

Someone has said that history is a record of the past, a knowledge of the present, and a prophecy of the future. In the preparation of this volume I have kept in mind this definition, and the aim of this book, as Macaulay expressed it, is "to make the past present, to bring the present near, to invest with the reality of human flesh and blood, beings whom we are too much inclined to consider as personified qualities."

Finally, it is to show that we are not superior to our ancestors. We live in a wonderful age. We naturally think it is more wonderful than any previous age. Be that as it may—our ancestors are largely responsible for the many improvements we enjoy. Our fathers worked for better things and made material progress; we started where they left off, but are yet far from the goal. We ought to be proud of the age and county in which we live, but we should not discredit the majestic work of our forebears. No man should look backward, as does the Chinaman, for the glory of ancestral worship, nor pause an instant in the real work of making a better world in which to live. One should only look back to catch the rays of the lamp of experience that light the way to greater achievements. The future is only judged by the past—and with this thought as a basis, I launch my "History of Izard County" with the hope that it may give courage to those who live, or have lived, in Izard County and nerve them for a greater and more successful work.

Sincerely,

KARR SHANNON.

TABLE OF CONTENTS

Part I—General History

PAGE

THE FIRST SETTLERS	1
OTHER EARLY SETTLERS	5
FIRST COUNTY SEATS	10
EARLY PERIODS OF HISTORY	16
EARLY MODES OF TRAVEL	20
TALES OF YORE	24
EARLY ACADEMIES	31
IZARD COUNTY SCHOOLS	38
IZARD COUNTY BANKING	45
IZARD COUNTY NEWSPAPERS	49
MELBOURNE, PRESENT COUNTY SEAT	53
CALICO ROCK, LARGEST TOWN	61
OTHER TOWNS	64

    Battles, Boswell, Brockwell, Creswell, Croker, Cross Roads, Day, Dolph, Forty-Four, Franklin, Gid, Gorby, Guion, Iuka, Jumbo, Knob Creek, LaCrosse, Lafferty, Larkin, Lunenburg, Mt. Pleasant, Mt. Olive, Myron, Newburg, Oxford, Pineville, Sage, Stella, Sylamore, Twin Creek, Violet Hill, Wideman, Wiseman, Zion.

IZARD COUNTY AND WARS	79
SINGINGS AND DANCES	84
CHURCHES AND PREACHERS	88
PRESENT COUNTY OFFICIALS	92
TENURE OF COUNTY OFFICERS	96
MODERN IZARD COUNTY	102
MISCELLANEA	105
GOVERNOR GEORGE IZARD	109

Part II—Biographies

JOHN C. ASHLEY	113
C. C. AYLOR	114
JAMES B. BAKER	114
DR. E. A. BAXTER	115
JOHN L. BLEDSOE	116
S. MARCUS BONE	117
P. A. BILLINGSLEY	117
COMDR. EDWARD BAXTER BILLINGSLEY	118
KIRBY BILLINGSLEY	119
DE E. BRADSHAW	120
ROBERT BURNS	121
R. L. BLAIR	123
THE BABER FAMILY	124

W. W. COPELAND	125
DAVE CRAIGE	125
J. ORVILLE CHENEY	126
MACK CYPERT	127
O. P. ESTES	127
R. J. ESTES	128
WILLIAM K. ESTES	129
JOSEPH T. GARNER	130
RANSOM GULLEY	130
J. DENTON GUTHRIE	131
F. M. HANLEY	131
JAMES A. HARRIS	133
J. A. HARRIS	133
H. H. HARRIS	134
SAMUEL BILLINGSLEY HILL	135
JEHOIDA JEFFERY	136
ROBERT EMMETT JEFFERY	137
D. O. JOHNSON	137
WILLIAM RICHARD KENDRICK	138
OWEN G. KENDRICK	139
R. L. LANDERS	139
E. G. LANDERS	140
J. HAYDEN LANDERS	140
THOMAS H. LINN	141
J. O. LINN	142
R. G. ("BOB") MILLER	143
THE MILLER MILITARY FAMILY	143
ARTHUR GRAY MASHBURN	144
E. E. MASHBURN	144
WILLIAM A. OLDFIELD	145
RICHARD H. POWELL	145
E. C. RODMAN	147
JAMES H. ROTEN	148
DR. HARLIN H. SMITH	148
A FAMILY OF DOCTORS	150
P. C. SHERRILL	150
MRS. NELLIE TREVATHAN	151
JOHN H. WOODS	152
JOHN P. WOODS	152
R. H. ("BOB") WOOD	153
JOHN Q. WOLF	153
THOMAS H. WREN	154

BRIEFS OF OTHERS 155
L. C. Gulley, Wilbur Gulley, E. E. Godwin, Dr. L. T. Evans, Dr. John Knox Freeman, C. O. Bradshaw, Fred Watkins, Boyce Stubblefield, H. F. Croom, Lee Rector, Van Johnson, J. T. Cone, Ewell Richardson, Dr. Otis McMurtrey, Dr. W. D. Hinson, Dr. C. E. Spann, Dr. Paul Jeffery, Dr. Arthur Billingsley, Dr. Charles Billingsley, Dr. J. L. Weathers, Dr. O. S. Woods, Dr. Myrlas Matthews, Dr. James Milburn, Dr. C. G. Hinkle, Earl R. Wiseman, Hanley Powell, Vernon Powell, W. E. Baxter, Austin Billingsley, Roscoe Billingsley, Ewell Billingsley, Frank Carder, Paul Morgan, Sam Rector, Paul Meers, D. E. McSpadden, Ray McSpadden, Coy Wilson, J. W. Williamson, W. T. McJunkins, Troy Gaston, Clyde Crutchfield, Kelsie Halbrook, H. H. Harris, E. R. Hall, Earl Landers, V. H. Regan, Davis Hill, L. U. Crutchfield, Freas Crutchfield, A. H. Benbrook, Brooke Wallace, Dr. James Dillard, Dr. Harber, Roy N. Jeffery, Dr. Tasso Edwards, John W. Taylor.

Part I
General History

THE FIRST SETTLERS

THE TERRITORY which comprises the County of Izard was a part of Louisiana and owned by France from the time LaSalle took possession in 1682 until the Louisiana Territory was ceded to Spain in 1762. In 1721 the territory was divided into nine "commands," each ruled by a "commandant." Arkansas was one of these commands. Spain ruled Louisiana until 1800 when she ceded it back to France. France then held possession until 1803 when the United States bought the entire territory. The population grew very slowly during the French and Spanish rule because the government was not such as would attract settlers. Before a man could settle in a province he had to obtain permission from a foreign official. A citizen was not allowed to go twenty miles from his home unless he got a passport describing the road he was to travel and the place he was to visit. Very few of the English or American people tried to make settlements across the Mississippi River against such restrictions. But after the United States came into possession of the Louisiana Territory it was settled rapidly by pioneers from east of the Mississippi River.

The early history of the county is shrouded in obscurity and the identity of the first white man to set foot on the soil of the present territory embraced by the county is not known. DeSoto visited this section in 1541 but whether he entered the county or not is not a matter of record. But there is some evidence to indicate that he did so, as the floods in the early part of 1927 uncovered several ancient burying grounds of the Indians, and in at least one of these were found Spanish coins bearing a date prior to DeSoto's explorations, which tends to prove that some of his men were buried in this county. If such should have been the case, he was probably the discoverer of what is now Izard County.

John Lafferty was the first white man of any permanent record to set foot on Izard County soil. He came with his father from Ireland when a mere boy, in 1760, and settled with the Irish clans in western North Carolina, in what was then Rowan County, now Rutherford. When he was 17 years of age he joined Capt. Smith's company in Col. Thomas Polk's regiment and served three years in the Revolutionary War. He enlisted June 10, 1776, and was mustered out June 15, 1779. He was connected with the Cherokee troubles in western North Carolina, which carried him into Tennessee. Here in the Cumberland district he married a Lindsey of pure Scotch blood.

John Lafferty lived for many years in Tennessee near the Kentucky line and all his children were born there. He became a rover of the grandest type. He hunted and trapped over a great part of Missouri, Louisiana, Arkansas and Kansas. He was on friendly terms with the Cherokee Indians of later days and with them hunted and trapped incessantly. In 1807 he brought his family to what is now called Lafferty Creek, in Izard County, and settled on the barrens in a little log hut, which in after days was one of the most famous in Arkansas. That cabin was then in Louisiana, but it existed through the days of the Missouri Territory, Arkansas Territory into the life of Arkansas State. The political divisions changed, but the little log cabin did not change with them.

At the time of Lafferty's settlement this was an exceptionally wild region. His closest neighbors were the Cadron family living where Conway now stands, over a hundred miles away. Most of this county at that time was prairie, with small trees, shrubbery and tall grass in places. Wild beast, such as the bear, panther and wolf, roamed the land and deer were plentiful. The land along Strawberry River was grown up in strawberry plants, hence its name. It is said that during the season in which this fruit ripened one could ride horseback only a short distance through the thick vines and the horse's legs would be bathed red with the abundant juice from the berries. Streams which are now filled with sand and only a few inches deep, were then deep enough to swim a horse.

In 1814 the tocsin of war called John Lafferty back to Tennessee, and he marched with Jackson to New Orleans, where he was wounded in the battle at that place. The war closed with this battle and he returned to his home in Izard County. But his wound was so severe that he died of its effects in his cabin home on Lafferty Creek in 1815. He was buried somewhere near the cabin.

In 1807 a caravan of Laffertys and Creswells left Tennessee with teams and wagons for Memphis where they built a boat and went down the Mississippi River to the mouth of Arkansas River. Here at the Post of Arkansas they purchased a supply of furniture, flour and salt. They then made their way up White River to the Paoli Fields.

John Lindsey Lafferty and Margaret Lafferty, a son and daughter of John Lafferty, were with this party. Elizabeth Lafferty, another daughter, married a man by the name of Kelley in Tennessee and formed another part of the caravan. Elizabeth Kelley died at the mouth of White River, where she was buried. Her husband kept on up the river with the Laffertys and died a few years after he reached the destination. This trip comprised six months. There was a young man with the party named Creswell, who on the 13th of March, 1813, married Margaret Lindsey. He was born in South Carolina in 1791 and died in Izard County October 1, 1844. His wife, Margaret, died February 23, 1868, and was buried near Old Philadelphia Church, now Larkin.

After the year 1810 quite a number of inhabitants made settlements in the White River section. Since there were no restrictions of law, almost every grade of character known among men was to be found here—hunters, stock raisers, horse thieves, murderers, and refugees from prisons east of the Mississippi. But ignorance was by no means the prevailing trait among the pioneers. Men of education and men who had seen better days were here. The valley of the White was not so much a scene of terror and bloodshed as it was a resting place for robbers while they preyed upon the early commerce of the Mississippi and the fine stock of Kentucky and Tennessee.

As early as 1810 Dan Wilson and his three sons, Dan, Dick and Jerome, settled at the mouth of Rocky Bayou, and here the first shadow of a town appeared in the county. It consisted of a blacksmith shop run by Dick Bean, a trading hut run by Bob Bean, and a pair of race tracks on a high sand bar. The inhabitants first cleared some land and made a crop, but the buffaloes and bears ate it up in the fall. Bob Bean ran a little trading boat up and down the river, exchanging salt, powder, whiskey and lead for buffalo hides, bear skins and peltry. The inhabitants had an occasional meet for horse racing at the place. On one of these occasions Dick Wilson's horse flew the track, ran under a leaning tree, and killed him. This settlement was near where Guion is now located, but there is not a trace of a single building left.

OTHER EARLY SETTLERS

The main points of location of the early settlers were, in general, along White and Strawberry rivers. Among the early settlers in the vicinity of the former stream were Henry and Elbert Benbrook, Daniel Hively, William Clifton, Daniel McCoy, Moses Bishop, George and James Partee, the Harrises, the Dillards and the Jefferys. Daniel Jeffery settled below what is now the town of Mt. Olive. Jehoida Jeffery, brother of Daniel, settled about a mile above, and James, another brother, near the mouth of Piney Creek. There were four of the Harris brothers, Augustus, Henry, James and Richard. Augustus located on the east side of the river, the others on the opposite side, now Stone County. Daniel Hively settled at the mouth of Piney Creek and built a water power mill, the first in the county. Among the first to locate on Strawberry River were the Simpsons, Billingsleys and Finleys. James Wren early resided at Lunenburg and John Gray located on Rocky Bayou near there.

Later came Robert and William Powell, Thomas Richardson, Samuel Bingham, William and James Woods, Col. Thomas Black, Jesse Hinkle, the Robinsons, the Walkers, the Lancasters, the Arnolds and the Watkinses. Both the early and the subsequent settlers came from Tennessee, although a few were from other states, mostly Southern states.

The early settlers of the White River country had very little trouble with the Indians. About the time that law was first enforced in the country, under the Territorial government of Missouri, the south side of the river from a point beginning at the mountain at the head of Hardin's Bluff, five miles above Batesville and extending up the river indefinitely, was ceded to the Cherokees, and known as the Cherokee grant, but for some cause they never moved to it. However, the Shawnee tribe was moved to this grant in 1819. These Indians were very quiet and not bad neighbors. The citizens made a profitable vocation trading with them, being allowed to trade in anything except spirituous liquors. It might be interesting to the reader to further pursue the history of the Shawnees while living on White River, they being the early settlers of the country along the river, but this volume is chiefly a history of men and women who have accomplished something in the making of Izard County, and we must be satisfied with an incident told here which will illustrate the Shawnees' ungovernable greed for whiskey.

William Clifton and Daniel McCoy had been down the river in a large canoe and were coming back by one of the small Indian settlements with a barrel of whiskey on board. The Indians were on the side of the river now known as Stone County, the other side being known as the "White Side." These men had some doubts of running the blockade past the Indians and laid their boat very near the white shore. The Indians began congregating on the opposite side and beckoning and calling them to come over, but the boat poled on. Soon, about twenty of them took to the water and started for the canoe. Clifton stayed with the boat, but his partner couldn't stand the storm and as the Indians laid hold of the boat McCoy jumped into the water and made it to the white side. Clifton wore out his canoe pole on them, but they dragged the boat to the opposite side of the river and rolled the barrel ashore. They then turned Clifton and his boat loose. Guns, knives, tomahawks and other weapons were put aside and the whole camp of Indians got drunk, women as well as men. There was a constant yell for two days and nights. A number of white men went to see them next day, but they had the precaution to go in squads sufficient to guard themselves against the drunken ones. Clifton went along and knocked down and stamped several of the drunken Indians.

The Watkinses settled in this county about 1844. They were great landowners and at times before the Civil War owned the greater part of the territory of the county. They also kept a large number of negro slaves. They established themselves in two main locations, one about two miles east of the present town of LaCrosse and the other about three miles south of the present location of Franklin.

Prior to 1848 there was no post office in Izard County except at New Athens (Mt. Olive), and the Watkinses had been getting their mail at Batesville, about thirty miles away. This distance was usually covered on horseback, and the trip meant two days of hard riding. There were no settlers along the routes, and wild animals lurked in the woods. Hence the rider had to be well armed and was usually accompanied by his dogs. If he happened to be after dark getting back home he was very likely to have a chase with a pack of wolves.

To improve such inconveniences, the Watkinses sought the establishment of two post offices at these two points of settlement. The settlement near the present town of Franklin was surrounded by numerous wild haw trees. The Watkins family had come from Franklin, Tennessee. Hence the name of Wild Haws for the location near the present site of Franklin and the name Franklin for the settlement near the place where LaCrosse now is, were submitted to the government as the names of the post offices at these places, respectively. The government got the names reversed, in some manner, and the former was named Franklin and the latter Wild Haws.

The little log house in which the second post office was

established in Izard County still stands near LaCrosse. Nearby is a large brick building which was erected by Owen Watkins in 1853. At that time it was the finest house of its kind in north Arkansas. Today it is in good repair and still used as a dwelling, owned by W. W. Fudge of Melbourne.

Supplies were first brought across the country from old Jacksonport landing, situated on White River about six miles above Newport. Later they were brought from Batesville. Still later they were landed about a mile above the location where the town of Guion now stands, and brought across the country in a northeastern direction to the towns of Wild Haws and Franklin. This place became known as Wild Haws landing.

Since most of Izard County at that time was prairie and there were but few large trees, the cattle business became very profitable. In the early "fifties" cattle buyers would buy up large droves of cattle and drive them across the country to Kansas City, which was the nearest railroad town. It would usually take about six months to make one of these trips and such would be accompanied by severe hardships and adventure. The hard ground covered with grass and leaves served as lodging places and wild game of the woods supplied the food. No doubt the sport of the trip compensated for all hardships.

The late Tom Watkins of LaCrosse states that during the early days of his father, the closest church house was at Batesville. He tells of one occasion when his father attended church there. The church was a large one-room structure built of logs. People for miles around came with their guns and dogs. Upon entering the house the guns were stacked against the wall. The preacher began his sermon and in a short time the dogs started a bear. The preacher said: "The service is adjourned in order that the men may kill that bear." They rolled out with alacrity, mounted their horses, pursued Bruin and killed him. He was hung to a tree ready for skinning and then they went back into the house where the preacher thanked God for men who knew how to shoot and women who knew how to pray, and finished his sermon.

FIRST COUNTY SEATS

IZARD COUNTY was the thirteenth county to be formed of the Territory of Arkansas, and was created by an Act of the Legislature October 27, 1825. It was named in honor of George Izard, governor of the territory.

It was formed of territory taken from Independence County and ran from the Independence County line to the Missouri line, touching Crawford County on the northwest corner where White River enters Arkansas. The river formed the southwestern boundary. Since that time territory has been cut off in the formation of Fulton, Baxter and Stone counties.

The original county seat was located on White River, at the mouth of Big North Fork, now in Baxter County. There stood the house of Jacob Wolf which was designated as the temporary seat of justice. The house was erected as a dwelling and trading post in 1809. Mr. Wolf ran a blacksmith shop, store and trading post there, and most of his dealings were with the Indians.

The building came into use as the county's courthouse in 1829. Prior to that time all official county business had been transacted in the circuit court. The old log structure still stands at its original location. In 1939 a W. P. A. project restored the building to its original appearance and established a museum in connection. It is now officially the Wolf Memorial.

Wolf Memorial, Izard county's first courthouse. Built in 1809, it is still in good repair.

This first county seat was known as the Town of Liberty. Jacob Wolf was about 60 years of age at the time and had been the chief influence in getting the county seat located there. He represented the county in the Territorial Legislature of 1827, the first after the county was organized.

John Dearman and James Jeffery were elected commissioners to locate a permanent county seat. They selected Athens, at the mouth of Piney Creek on White River, about three miles below the present site of Calico Rock, and in 1830 the county seat was moved to this location where it remained until 1836 when it was moved to Mt. Olive, six miles farther down the river.

When created, the county was sparsely settled. Old Jacksonport in Jackson County had been the chief landing place of the emigrants. Supplies were brought across the county from there in ox wagons. In 1830 fifty families settled in the county, and the population that year reached 1,266. After steamboating began on White River as far up as Batesville, which was in 1831, emigration continued to increase.

In 1830 the county seat of Athens consisted of one store, a blacksmith shop and a tavern. Livingston and Wolf had a saw and grist mill in operation, the only one in the county. A courthouse was soon erected. It was a one-story frame building, twenty feet square with a door in the east and one in the west side. Legend has it that the woodpeckers were so bad in the vicinity they almost ate up the courthouse during the first two years until a bounty of five cents a head was offered by a public-spirited levying court.

When the courthouse was erected at Athens no provision was made for heating the room, so late in the fall it was decided to build a chimney. A meeting was called for the purpose of making the necessary arrangements. At this meeting some extravagant persons who were in favor of progress advocated the building of a stone chimney. They declared that old Peter Young and Sol Hess were both skilled in this kind of work and could build a chimney of stone that would look much better than one built of "stick and clay" and would last forever. Jim Creswell took a very decided stand against the motion, and in bursts of oratory, declared that he was not in favor of "grinding the people to death with taxes." He also said he was in favor of holding to old landmarks and building chimneys of stick and dirt as all had been accustomed to, and which would be much cheaper. The arguments of this staunch servant of the people were too logical to be disregarded—so the first courthouse ever built in what is now Izard County had a stick and dirt chimney.

The tradition of history has become somewhat indistinct by the lapse of time, but old settlers handed down information to the effect that before the town was abandoned as the seat of justice it maintained several dwellings, two or three stores, a tavern and probably a church house. But today there is no town at the site, neither are there any signs that there ever was a town there.

The courthouse in the new county seat at Mt. Olive was a two-room log structure, and an administration had come into power with so little mercy for the taxpayers that a stone chimney was built at the time the house was erected. Extravagance continued and about three years later the log building was weatherboarded.

This house was so substantial that it stood for over a hundred years. After the county seat was moved from Mt. Olive in 1875 the building was used as a dwelling many years. It finally came into use as a barn by a resident of the town, and was not torn down until about 1938.

The first county officials of the county were J. P. Houston,

HISTORY OF IZARD COUNTY

Izard County's courthouse when the county seat was at Mt. Olive.

clerk; John Adams, sheriff. These two men were elected in 1825 to serve terms of two years. Both were re-elected in 1827. No other offices appeared until 1829 when Matthew Adams was chosen judge and H. C. Roberts coroner. J. P. Houston and John Adams were elected to a third term to their respective offices. Jesse Adams became clerk in 1830 and served two years. J. P. Houston was again chosen in 1832 and served until 1838. W. B. Carr was elected the first county treasurer in 1836 and served until 1838 when he was succeeded by A. Creswell, who also served one term. William Clement, the first county surveyor, was elected in 1830 and served one term of two years. The county was then without a surveyor until 1835 when A. Adams was elected. A county tax assessor was not chosen until as late as 1868 when P. F.

Heasley was elected. He was succeeded two years later by W. O. Dillard.

In the biennial report of Secretary of State Jim B. Higgins, 1925-26, a summary of the changes of the boundaries of Izard County since its formation in 1825 is given as follows: "Western boundary line extended, October 13, 1827; part of the Indian purchase added October 22, 1828; between Independence and Izard defined, November 5, 1831; between Conway and Izard, November 5, 1831; southern boundary established, November 11, 1833; line between Independence defined, February 21, 1838, and December 14, 1838, and December 21, 1840; western boundary defined, December 24, 1840, act March 1873; between Baxter and Fulton, defined, February 17, 1875; between Sharp changed, March 9, 1877."

EARLY PERIODS OF HISTORY

A. C. JEFFERY, in an issue of *The Melbourne Clipper*, published in 1877, gives a sketch of the early history of Izard County as follows:

"The society and habits of a country are continually undergoing a change. These changes through force of circumstances are very suddenly precipitated upon a country, while at others they are so gradual that they are scarcely noticeable by a careless observer. From our personal observations we have thought proper to divide those changes into four decades or periods in which the mould of society was materially changed in each period, allowing five years to change from one period to another.

"For a time from the beginning of white settlements in the valley of White River until 1815 to 1820, we will name the first period, allowing these latter five years to effect the revolution. During the first period the inhabitants were a promiscuous mass of hunters, trappers, stock raisers, murderers, robbers, runaway rogues and bankrupts. This first period found the valley of the White River with quite a run of emigrants without the restrictions of law or the fear of God before their eyes, and every man was his own law. It must be observed, however, that the predominance of sterling intellect prevailed among this class of pioneers, accompanied in many instances with education. Of the prominent families composing the mass we will mention the Yocums, the Friends, the Bryants, the Trimble brothers, the Hawthorns, the Ramseys, the Partees, the Irons and the Carters, in advance of whom was the Falenash family. The Yocums and Friends were perhaps North Carolinians, the Cokers and Sneeds, east Tennesseeans, Ben Bryant, a Portugee, and the Trimbles, Hawthorns, Ramseys and Partees were Kentuckians.

"Many of these early pioneers received the ushering of the second period with acclamations of joy and fell into the great march of civilization under the law, while others, 'preferring darkness rather than light, because their deeds were evil,' like owls and bats at the approach of day, flew to the rocks and caves to hide themselves.

"Of the very first standard bearers of law and order who planted their colors on the banks of White River, may be mentioned Rev. George Gill, Robert Livingstone, Col. Stewart. Judge Jeffery, Col. John Miller, Jess Miller, Capt. Jess Bean. Bob Bean, Mark Bean, and Dick Bean. They have all run their race and sleep with their fathers. This inauguration of the second period in society in the valley of White River was very rapidly reinforced by such families as the Wolfs, the Adams, the Hartgraves, the Talberts, the Langstons, the Hightowers, the Lancasters, the Creswells, the Harrises, the Allens, the Finleys, the Walkers, the Wrens, Dick Hutchinson and a host of others. This tide of emigration continued to flow with great rapidity into the valley until about 1830, when the influx seemed to abate. This was, no doubt, on account of the opening of new fields in western Tennessee, in Mississippi and finally in eastern Texas. These early settlements were generally confined to the river and the water courses until they became well settled. It will be observed that these inhabitants were nearly all from Virginia, the Carolinas, Georgia, Kentucky and Tennessee. With a great similarity in their habits, manners, and customs the most of these pioneers were in easy circumstances. Society naturally took a mould of its own throughout the valley, which lasted unbroken until the end of the second period, which to some extent surrendered up its existence from the year 1845 to 1850.

"The third period in the model of society, and more especially in Izard County, lasted until the year of 1860 to 1865, from which time the county underwent another great change in society, which carried us into the fourth period. These changes in society, no doubt, were often for the better, but we regret to have to say, were not always so, and as the purest days of the government of the United States was in its early existence in like manner. We do claim the purest days of the valley of White River, and more especially Izard County, principally included in this second period of her existence.

"In these golden days the country people were engaged in the cultivation of the soil, the raising of fine stock, wheat, corn, pork and bacon, and beef cattle, accumulated in large quantities, which found a market in New Orleans by being floated away in flat-bottomed boats. This was done by the farmer himself or by the river trader, as he chose, and supplies brought back by means of keel boats.

"In these days of chivalry in the territory, and more especially in the valley of White River, what men said they would do, they intended to do. The legal ability of the territory was composed of such men as the Johnsons of Kentucky, Chester Ashley, Robert Crittendon, Townsend Dickinson, the Conways, David Walker, and a host of others who would compare favorably with any place or any time.

"The valley of White River had such legal ability as Dickinson, Dave Walker, Desha, Searcy, Pope, Denton, Curran, and finally William Byers, which composed as ably as this country ever produced. After the year 1827 a revival of religion commenced under the preaching of the Baptist, the Methodist and the Cumberland Presbyterian churches, which continued to spread until it covered the whole inhabited valley of White River, and until almost everybody was either religious or strictly moral. The ministerial ability in those days seemed to be of the highest grade of wisdom, education and deep piety. It was not the custom in those days to preach denominations to hell and let the sinner go scot-free. This gospel spread showed no signs of relaxation until about the close of the second period. In those old-time days the boys and young men didn't all betake themselves to professions, and only such beardless boys were called doctors or lawyers who after strict trial and due examination were found worthy. During the purity of the second period the various political interests hunted up and put forward their best man for office. Canvasses were generally conducted with decency and respectability. A want of ability, drunkenness and blackguardism were generally invited to take a back seat by the people at the polls, and such epithets as 'liar,' 'thief,' 'robber,' or 'swindler,' if applied in a canvass, meant either blood or backout at once.

"During these palmy days of this second period a pictorial magazine and a fashion plate were not a necessity in every well regulated family in the country. We remember to have seen young ladies who were able and did dress in the finest apparel, who were heir to their thousands, appear at church in afternoon service, attired in goods of their own manufacture, displaying their rich colors of turkey red and blue. They were beautiful 'for a' that.' "

EARLY MODES OF TRAVEL

WE WHO LIVE in Izard County at present find ourselves living in a progressive age. We have beautiful homes with average conveniences, and are surrounded by fertile farms and thriving little villages and towns. There are schools, churches and stores within reach of all. There are mail routes, public roads and highways extending to every section of the county. Automobiles have become a common mode of travel, and the White River Division of the Missouri Pacific Railroad puts us within easy reach of the commercial world. We get news from Little Rock the same day it is published, and it is not an uncommon sight for an airplane to soar over.

Such excellent conditions, however, have not always existed in Izard County. Church houses are still standing in various localities which were at one time surrounded by nothing but ox wagons on the day of worship. The man with a team of horses was usually a man of wealth, and the man who had a buggy or hack was really a man of dignity. But inconvenience of travel did not bar anyone from the church door. People came for miles in ox wagons, on horseback, and on foot; some of them as far as twenty miles. Now at a community meeting of any kind in most any part of the county there are always a number of cars on the ground, but few, if any, horses.

There was a time when there were no mail routes in the county. Some of the pioneers got their mail at Batesville.

HISTORY OF IZARD COUNTY

Later, a mail route was established from Walnut Ridge, in Lawrence County, to Harrison, in Boone County, a distance of 160 miles. Important on this route were such towns as Poughkeepsie, Evening Shade, LaCrosse, Melbourne, Mt. Olive, Pineville, Iuka, Mountain Home and Yellville. This route was divided into a number of sections and covered once a day on horseback, one carrier leaving Harrison and another Walnut Ridge at the same time. This was a very dangerous journey for the horseman. He had to go well armed. Not only did he carry weapons for the purpose of defense against the wild animals that roved the country at that time, but as protection against robbers. Very frequently the mail carrier was ordered off his horse and the pouches searched for valuables by a gang of outlaws.

In 1880 a railroad was constructed to Batesville and then the mail route was changed from Batesville through Izard County and on northwest over about the same country. No mail boxes had yet been patented and the mail carrier equipped himself with a horn which he blew before he arrived at a post office, so that everyone in the surrounding country would know when to come to the office for mail. Postage was high, often as much as twenty-five cents for a single letter. This was usually paid by the person receiving the letter instead of the sender. There was no such thing as parcel post at that time, and only letters and small papers could be sent by mail.

In 1884 a railroad was started from Batesville to Carthage, Missouri. This road was constructed to Cushman, Independence County, and there was discontinued, even to the present day. But on this date the mail route was changed from Cushman to Melbourne. This was only a trail that went to Melbourne, and from there to other parts of the county. Another route was established to Lunenburg, via Adler and Gid. In the meantime, some mail was carried by steamboat up White

HISTORY OF IZARD COUNTY

River and a post office was established near the present site of Guion, and was named Louis, but the steamboat service was so irregular that it was soon discontinued.

In 1902 another effort was made to establish a railroad from Batesville to Missouri. This time the road was started up White River. The road was constructed to Mt. Olive and there the company decided it would not be a paying proposition and gave up the project. A few months later construction was again begun and the road was completed to Carthage.

Now we have about fifty miles of railroad in Izard County winding along parallel with White River on one side and the high bluffs on the other. Such beautiful scenery is a rarity and a paradise to many business men and women who take this route to spend their vacations among the Ozark Mountains. We now have regular passenger and freight service on this road, and a number of little towns have grown up along the way.

The completion of this railroad settled the mail and freight question for the country along White River in the southwestern part of the county. A mail route was established from Guion to Melbourne about the year 1903, and over this route mail was carried to other parts of the county. Freight was hauled in wagons from Guion to Melbourne, a distance of twelve miles. The road followed Rocky Bayou Creek to Lunenburg, a distance of some seven miles, and crossed the creek thirty-two times. Mail service and freighting were fairly regular in spite of the bad roads, except in the early spring when most of the rains fell. During this season the creek would overflow, washing out the road and putting traffic at a standstill for days at a time.

In the summer of 1925 the Batesville-Mammoth Spring highway was completed. In Izard County it touches Mt. Pleasant, Stella, Sage, Melbourne, Brockwell (which grew up after the completion of the highway) and Oxford. A short while before this a highway was completed from Calico Rock to where Brockwell is now located. This road is also a hard-surfaced road and has concrete culverts. The people of Calico Rock supervised the building of this road and it was financed by the sale of bonds. It has since been taken over by the state and has been extended east to the Sharp County line. The Batesville-Mammoth Spring highway was a state highway from the beginning and is kept up by state funds.

In 1926 the mail route was changed again and now runs from Batesville to Mammoth Spring, serving the towns along the highway.

Since 1930 a state highway has been built from Melbourne to Sylamore, and another from near Sage to Sidney. Several hundred miles of good county roads were built during "W. P. A. Days."

TALES OF YORE

ABOUT THE YEAR 1830 there was a desperate character named Abb Garrison who roamed the valley of White River from head to mouth. He killed a number of men in different localities and was a great terror to the early settlers of Izard County. About three miles south of the mouth of North Fork River, then Izard County, there lived a man named Bevins who was a rather harmless man and had a large family of small children. Abb Garrison on passing there one day, called Bevins to the fence, shot him dead among his children, and with a hearty laugh, rode off as if he had played some good joke. It was said that he never had any provocation for this inhuman deed. But he finally met his fate a few months later at Montgomery's Point, near the mouth of White River. Here he met a man by the name of Combie. Each had threatened the other's life. When they met Garrison attempted to draw his pistol, but it was fastened in the case, and before he could get it out Combie seized him by the collar with one hand and ran a Bowie knife through his body. Garrison fell dead on the spot. The news of the killing was received with joy throughout the White River valley.

Rev. John Milligan, a pioneer preacher of Izard County, was a very old man at the beginning of the Civil War. Up to that time he had accumulated considerable wealth. While his older sons were battling for their country under Dixie's flag, Rev. Milligan, his wife and a half-grown son remained

HISTORY OF IZARD COUNTY

at home near the present town of Mt. Olive. While this old man and woman and their son were sitting around the fire one night, four young men abruptly thrust themselves into the room, threw their pistols in the old man's face, and demanded his money. Without betraying much alarm the old man remonstrated with such logic that the robbers turned from him to his son, threw a skillet in the fire, heated it, stripped the boy's shoes off his feet and swore that they would burn the boy's feet off to his knees if the father didn't show the money. The old man bore it until he saw the boy's feet almost scorching against the hot skillet and heard his screams. He then commanded them to stop and immediately took a light and showed them where to dig in a stable. They dug up a vessel of gold and silver. The old man asked them what kind of excuse they would render at the Bar of Judgment, but they snatched the container of the money, blew out the light and disappeared in the darkness.

The following story appeared in *The Melbourne Clipper* in 1877, written by A. C. Jeffery:

"About the year 1811, the Trimble brothers, Lewis Partee, Tom and John Ramsey, and Andy and Thomas Hawthorn made their way from South Carolina to the White River valley. The most daring of this crew was said to be Bill Trimble. It seems that a man by the name of Grant followed him from Kentucky. Keeping himself disguised, he soon got very intimate with Bill Trimble. They made arrangements to go down the river on a hunt in a canoe. The first day out they stopped at Hawthorn's for dinner (about three miles below the present town of Calico Rock). Trimble was drinking and Grant pretended to be. While there Hawthorn's mother, a very old woman, cautioned him to be careful, as she was uneasy for his welfare from a dream she had the night before. There was a rock standing in a field as large as an ordinary horse, and she said that she dreamed that she saw an owl sitting on the rock and that it flew down and she went to it, and it was Bill Trimble.

"They left Hawthorn's place late in the evening and went to where two Carter women lived. After dark Grant professed to be pretty drunk, picked up his gun and stepped out of the house, and declared he was going on that night. But Trimble followed him out of the house and prevailed upon him to go back, which he did, but left his gun out of doors. He soon made another attempt to go, and took Trimble's gun with him. Trimble, followed him to the door, trying to get him back, when Grant shot him dead with his own gun.

"The women were greatly alarmed, but he went back into the house to quiet them. He told them that he would not harm them for the world, and that his name was Grant. He had not told his real name before. He also told them that Trimble had abused his wife in Kentucky.

"Each of the men had their rifles named, Grant calling his 'Jack of Diamonds,' and Trimble had named his 'Sweet Lips.' Grant told the women that 'Sweet Lips' had spoken a big word and that 'Jack of Diamonds' would speak another soon. He turned Trimble over to see that he was dead and bade the women goodnight. 'Sweet Lips' remained a relic in Izard County for many years.

"Grant was not heard of again until he got to Wat Trimble's, at the head of Trimble's Island, in lower White River, where he landed, went up to the house and found him almost dead with disease and unable to walk. Grant told Wat his name and that he had killed his brother Bill, and that he had stopped to kill him also, but that his Maker was killing him fast enough and that he would let him alone. He got into his canoe and was never heard of on White River again. From some cause—superstition, perhaps—they carried Bill Trimble back and buried him where his mother saw the owl alight on the ground."

James P. Houston, Izard County's first clerk, was a brother of the illustrious Sam Houston, former congressman, governor of Tennessee and first governor of Texas.

Sam was a great friend to the Indians, and lived with them after their own fashion for several years. One of the chiefs adopted him as his son. But Sam left the Indians, served in the army for some years and then, in civilian life again, was elected district attorney, congressman, and governor of Tennessee.

In 1829 he married a young lady who was a member of a prominent Tennessee family. Three months later his wife left him for reasons unknown. He immediately resigned as governor, left Tennessee and went to Arkansas where his former friends, the Cherokees, had removed and lived for about three years.

While in the state, he visited his brother, James, at the old county seat of Athens, in Izard County. Tradition has it that the two brothers were far from cordial in their meeting. Shortly afterward, James suggested that they step out the back of the courthouse under the big oak. A few minutes later loafers about the village heard some loud quarreling. James firmly ordered his brother to leave the state and never return.

Sam left for Texas where, at the outbreak of the Mexican War, he was made commander-in-chief of the Texan army, and, after Texas gained her independence from Mexico, he became the first governor.

Nobody ever knew what the trouble was between James and Sam Houston.

Back in the early days of Melbourne when an open saloon operated just off the southwest corner of the square where the switchboard office is now located, the situation sometimes got wet and stormy.

A man who answered to the name of Scraggs was a perpetual patron of the saloon and, when he imbibed to capacity, became rancorous and bloodthirsty. Often when wildly drunk, he would pull his gun and everybody would take to cover, including the bartender.

On one of these occasions he shot up the saloon and then went about the streets threatening anybody who dared to show his head. The entire populace went to their homes and locked themselves inside. Scraggs was in full charge of the town and was the only evidence of life about the place.

This was a midafternoon of a hot summer's day. Dr. E. A. Baxter, a young practitioner at the time, had been out on a call and was just riding his horse into town when he was hailed by Scraggs with: "I'm the best goddamn man in town!"

The young doctor quickly answered: "I believe every word of it, and I'm next best."

Dr. Baxter told the writer this incident several years before he died. He said he knew Scraggs was drunk but didn't know he was on one of his super-benders and had scared everybody out of town. The doctor admitted that had he known the circumstances he might have been a little more cautious with his response. "But Scraggs must have been in the process of sobering," he added, "because he offered no fight; he just laughed and walked off, and I rode on home."

Murders have never been a fad in Izard County. There have been very few killings. Some of the guilty persons may have suffered slight punishment for taking the life of another, in the opinion of some citizens. But in almost every case they have been given a good round of "court procedure."

That is, all except in two instances in which the identity of the groups of killers was an open secret, known to practically everybody—and nothing was ever done about it. The informant, who hands the stories down, recalls that in the days of the reconstruction period immediately after the Civil War to keep one's mouth shut paid good dividends in health, happiness and general well being.

Shortly after the Civil War a resident of near Lunenburg, a Mr. Nail, had been robbed of a considerable amount of money. At about the same time a suspicious stranger appeared at the town. A group of citizens, some of whom were later prominent in the business and professional affairs of the county, according to a story that was familiar years ago, took the stranger in custody for the purpose of questioning him. He proved to be a stubborn and uncommunicative chap. As an inducement toward supplying wanted information a rope was placed about his neck and passed over the limb of a sycamore tree. It would be drawn tight so that the stranger's toes would barely touch the ground and at his signal would be relaxed, but on each such occasion he would refuse to talk. It was decided to draw the rope as tightly as possible with safety to scare the man into loquaciousness. But the questioners miscalculated their strength and the man's neck was snapped. He was buried in a grave from which a northerner had been exhumed a short time before. No investigation or arrest was ever made.

Another case occurred about the same time and falls in the same category. A gang of horse thieves had been especially active around Melbourne. While a vigilante group, working on the case, had never been able to apprehend the rustlers they had sighted them on several occasions and had recognized a young man named Victor. When the thievery continued the vigilantes captured Victor and he was hanged about a mile and a half south of Melbourne. They placed him on a horse with the noose about his neck and the rope tied to a limb. When no member of the posse would lead the horse from beneath Victor a bundle of fodder was waved from a distance. When the horse went to the feed the victim was executed. The posse was said to have been made up of some of the county's most prominent citizens.

Another murder mystery was related to the writer by the late T. H. Linn, who said he heard the story often when a young man.

A man named Halcomb, about whom little was known, lived near Guion. One morning his dead body was found tied to a rail fence about two miles north of that place. Relatives were notified and they buried him alongside the fence where he was found. The killing was a real mystery, Mr. Linn said, and nothing about the case was ever brought to light.

P. A. Billingsley, former Izard County sheriff, relates an incident about his grandmother's return to her home at Violet Hill from a visit with relatives in the vicinity where Guion is now located back in the early days when wild beast lurked in the woods.

Some negro slaves took her and her children in a boat up White River to the mouth of Twin Creek. Here they mounted a horse for the long trip of about twenty miles across a scantily settled country. The woman had her baby in her lap, and the three-year-old boy behind her.

On the way a large panther followed them and tried to jump on the horse, but the horse would jump aside as the beast would spring, causing him to miss. This continued for six miles up the hollow until they reached the Thompson settlement where several men armed with guns set out to kill the panther. They, with their dogs, gave chase and soon the beast took refuge in a cave where one of the hunters crawled in and shot it by the glare of its eyes.

The panther measured 10 feet from tip of nose to tip of tail. It had been in the section for years and had killed many calves, pigs and hogs.

EARLY ACADEMIES

SOON AFTER the close of the Civil War the citizens of Izard County came to see the need of higher education and as a result two academies were very successfully conducted for a number of years at Old Philadelphia and LaCrosse. Also some academic work was carried on at Mt. Pleasant, then Barren Fork, for about twelve years, supervised chiefly by I. K. Hooper. There is no better record of the North Arkansas Academy, held at Philadelphia, than the one found in a little pamphlet written by B. A. Spradlin in 1920. The booklet is called *The Philadelphians* and the sketch reads as follows:

"A few years after the close of the Cvil War, several planters from 'the bottoms' in Jackson and Woodruff counties moved to 'the hills' of Izard County, to find health, homes and educational facilities. Prominent among those who thus settled at Philadelphia, near the old Philadelphia spring, were William Purcell, John Sorrels, John Tarkington, Augustus Spradlin and Rufus Kerchevol; and with the cooperation of several former citizens of the vicinity, they began at once to look after the establishment of a permanent school. Among the latter may be mentioned, as the most active, Curtis Stevens, Bob Harris, Henry Williams, John Hare, and James Hill.

"Having at their disposal a two-story log house which had been erected some twenty years before for lodge and school purposes, they decided to secure teachers at once, begin

Old Barren Fork Academy, Mt. Pleasant.

school in this building, and chip in for the erection of a commodious school building. To this end two brothers, Joe F. and John W. C. Gardner, were induced to move up from Jackson County, where they had been engaged in teaching, and take charge. This they did in 1870, opening with as many pupils as could be accommodated with teachers and room provided.

"Thus passed the first year, the Gardners teaching and the patrons building; and when time for the second school year to begin, the new house was ready. Ransom Gulley, also from Jackson County, was added to the teaching force, a music department, with Miss Prussia Gardner (afterwards Mrs. W. E. Davidson) in charge, and all went 'merry as a wedding bell.' The enrollment for this year was about 150. As soon as it became known that the school was to be on a permanent basis, there set in an influx of newcomers, chiefly from the lower counties; and there was a boom of buying and building.

"After the third year J. F. Gardner retired for other pursuits. Then Ransom Gulley (about 1877) retired to enter upon the practice of law and engage in farming, which left the management with J. W. C. Gardner, who remained in charge with such assistants as he chose to employ from time to time until 1905, when the school, as a high school, was discontinued. During this interval, however, between 1877 and 1905 he was connected with other schools: one year at LaCrosse, two at Melbourne, and three at Salem, in Fulton County, the Philadelphia school being at these times somewhat irregular and under various teachers, and not doing high school work.

"About 1887 or perhaps 1888 the school building burned, rendering it necessary to carry on work in the church house for something more than a year while the neighbors could chip in and build again. This time it was deemed best to select another site; and the spot where the old house had stood was chosen, the old building having been purchased and converted into a barn by John Sorrells. So it came about that the school died in 1905 on the spot, where in 1870, it had its origin—just across the way from the famous old Methodist Church, which some sixty years before had been erected for neighborhood worship, and had been used as such by all denominations."

It is said that frequently a stranger passed through the neighborhood and inquired how far it was to Philadelphia. The North Arkansas Academy for years held the reputation of doing the best school work for several counties. Naturally one looked for a town; but he only found a crossroad, a church, a spring, a few houses near, and a school building in the background. The school was the community center. The teacher lived on his farm near the schoolhouse and conducted or influenced all community enterprises. His authority was seldom questioned and he was a leader in the community, as well as a neighbor.

The record of this academy will be incomplete without giving a sketch of the life of the founder and teacher, J. W. C. Gardner. He was born May 28, 1850, in Tennessee where he was chiefly educated at West Tennessee College, now Southern Baptist University. In 1868 he came to Jackson County, Arkansas. He left college in the middle of his senior year and married instead of taking his degree of Bachelor of Arts.

In 1873 Mr. and Mrs. Gardner established a home in sight of the old log schoolhouse in Philadelphia, where they resided almost constantly till 1905, becoming the parents of ten children.

Beginning at the age of eighteen in Jackson County, near Jacksonport, Mr. Gardner taught almost all of every year

HISTORY OF IZARD COUNTY

until 1905. Since that time he taught only one three-month term in the public school in his old home district in Jackson County. Besides ordinary school work he was county examiner of Izard County for a total incumbency of about fifteen years, with an interval or two out. He was employed by the state superintendent to hold twenty-day normals in Izard, Randolph, Jackson, and Fulton counties back in the "90's." In addition to these activities, he served Izard County in the Legislature of 1877. Mr. Gardner died January 25, 1944.

The LaCrosse Collegiate Institute was founded by M. Shelby Kennard at LaCrosse in the year 1868. It continued in the building in which it was founded until the tornado of 1883, when the building was destroyed. Soon after, a new building was erected which still stands. The history of this academy dates to 1902 when it seems to have died a natural death.

Prof. Kennard was the controlling factor of this school throughout most of its history, but he received the aid of such men as Prof. Pomroy, Mr. Gardner, and H. C. Tipton, who was at one time State Treasurer. These teachers did a high grade of work, emphasizing culture and character-building. The teaching was thorough, correct and up-to-date. As people gained knowledge they also acquired strength of character. The teachers were sincere in moral precept and example. The essential elements of an education in this school were honesty, integrity and industry. Greek, Latin and mathematics were the chief subjects of the course of study. This academy established a wide reputation and drew students from all sections of the state.

The school offered opportunities for special culture in literary societies and debating clubs. Like the school at Philadelphia, the social entertainments consisted largely of holiday parties of the boys and girls where games amused and pleased. Summer-time picnics, fishing trips and campings-out also played a part in the wholesome recreation of all.

One cannot attempt to picture the real value of this school without giving a sketch of the founder.

Michael Shelby Kennard was born in Sumpter County, Alabama, February 12, 1833. His father was a native of Tennessee and his mother a native of Georgia. He graduated from the University of Alabama in 1852, receiving the Master of Arts degree. In the winter of 1852 he began teaching school in West Feliciana Parish. He taught in public and private schools in Natchez, Mississippi, one year and in his spare time studied law.

He came to Arkansas in July, 1854, settling at Batesville. He lived at Batesville until 1868 when he moved to LaCrosse where he established the school. In 1871 he moved to Warren, Bradley County, and lived there until 1876, at which date he returned to LaCrosse to live.

He was admitted to the bar in Batesville in 1856. Soon after, he was induced to take charge of *The Independent Balance,* a newspaper started by Judge Byers at Batesville in 1857. He bought the paper in 1858 and devoted himself earnestly to the work of building a first-class paper. At this time he gave up the practice of law and never again gave it any attention. The *Balance* was continued until January, 1862, and was one of the most prominent papers in the state.

In 1859 he was elected mayor of Batesville. In 1860, with Capt. C. C. Donley, editor of *The Gazette,* and James B. Keats, of Little Rock, he was a delegate to the Baltimore Convention in 1861.

In the Civil War he joined Sweet's Texas Regiment. In 1862 he was made adjutant to this regiment and was captured with the regiment at Arkansas Post in January, 1863, after which he was held prisoner for several months. Afterwards he served as adjutant in McCoy's Brigade, raised in 1864.

At the close of the war he decided to devote the rest of his life to the profession of teaching. While in Bradley County he was county superintendent of schools in 1874. He married at Saunderville, Tennessee, in 1852, and by this marriage there were eight children. In 1889 he moved to Smithville, Lawrence County, and became head of an institute there. Later he was president of Mountain Home College, in Baxter County, for several years. He died in 1902.

In 1866 the Arkansas Legislature granted a charter to the Mt. Olive Male and Female Academy. A two-story brick building was erected for the institution, which continued operation until about time the county seat was moved from Mt. Olive to Melbourne. Several good teachers taught in the academy, but the outstanding terms seem to have been held in 1871-75 when Prof. John Stackpole of New York headed the school, and was assisted by two other teachers from the state of New York—J. Smothers and John Songers. One year the enrollment in the upper grades was 45. Of this number, 30 were Jefferys. Prof. Stackpole taught two terms.

Teachers and boarding students stayed at "The Mt. Olive Tavern" which was operated by a Mrs. Compton, whose son, T. S. Compton, now lives at Batesville. This was a very popular tavern in county-seat days, also being the lodging place of the circuit judge, prosecuting attorney and other officials during court sessions.

IZARD COUNTY SCHOOLS

IN THE EARLY DAYS of Izard County the children had very poor educational advantages. This was not because our forefathers did not believe in education, but because they had no money to establish schools and were too busy building and preparing homes to give proper attention to the schooling of their children. Then, too, the county was so sparsely settled that it was almost impossible to organize schools.

The first elementary schools were private schools. The teacher canvassed the community with a written contract stating the terms under which the school would be taught, and the people subscribed pupils at one or more dollars each per month. He took part of his pay in board at the homes of the pupils, and was frequently paid in pork, meal, sugar, or other acceptable produce. The preacher was often the teacher.

When a neighborhood contained a sufficient number of children to warrant the establishment of a school, the pioneers would cooperate in the erection of a schoolhouse at some central point where it would be convenient for the greatest number of pupils. The house would consist of one large room built of logs. A door would be cut at one end of the building and a huge fireplace at the other end. A window, two or three feet square, would be placed in each side of the house.

There were no varnished desks in those days. The school

furniture was "home-made" and scant in quantity. A plank pushed between two logs of the wall served as a desk. The benches were made of split logs placed on wooden pegs. In some districts the builders were thoughtful enough to make these benches of different heights, to accommodate children of different ages. But usually they were made the same size, standing about three feet high. From these seats dangled the children's legs.

Many pupils came on horseback from a distance of five miles or more, bringing feed for their horses and lunch for themselves, remaining "from early morn till dewey eve." The teacher also brought his dinner and the noon hour was the most important period of the school day.

Recess was held in both morning and afternoon and the noon hour was also used for recreation. The favorite game in the summer was ball, or "scrub," and that in winter was "base." The teacher usually participated in the games with the children.

The pioneer teacher was rarely an academic graduate, but if he knew enough to "set copy" for the pupils, and "do all the sums" in the arithmetic, he was qualified to teach. However, one qualification he must possess—physical strength to hold the unruly and boisterous boys in subjection. At the opening of the term, the teacher would frequently bring into the schoolroom a bundle of "hickories," which would be displayed in a conspicuous place as a sort of prophylactic for all disorders.

These rural schools seldom attempted to teach more than the Three R's—Reading, 'Riting and 'Rithmetic. There was no such thing as a uniform system of textbooks, authorized by a board of education. About the only book with which the children were supplied was Webster's Blue Back Speller —still remembered by many of the older men and women of the county. Other books were McGuffey's and Wilson's readers and Ray's arithmetics. Grammar was rarely taught. If geography were taught, it was confined to the geography of the United States.

More attention was given to orthography than to any other branch. The spelling classes recited at least twice a day. The class stood in a row and spelled orally. The chief aim of the student was to "turn down" as many of the class as possible and receive "head-marks." At the close of the term of school the one receiving the greatest number of head-marks was awarded a prize of some kind. Friday afternoons were devoted chiefly to spelling matches. Frequently out of these schools grew the oldtime neighborhood spelling matches, in which young and old took part. The people for miles around gathered on Saturday night at the old school-house. All those present who wished to participate were arrayed in two opposing lines. Then the teacher "gave out" the words, first to one side and then the other. Each speller who missed a word took his seat. Interest grew as the lines thinned, excitement ran high, and there was great applause for the victor. The champion speller of the neighborhood had the importance in those days that the best baseball or basketball player has today.

Community literary societies were also big attractions. These societies were open to everyone in the neighborhood. The programs were often of several hours duration and consisted of everything from readings and declamations to debates and bogus courts. Happily some of the rural schools of the county still maintain such community centers, but the spirit is probably not as great as in former times.

There was not any general or state-wide attempt to establish and organize a public school system until 1843, when an act "to establish a system of common schools in the State of Arkansas" was passed. This act provided for the organization by the County Court of townships upon request for the administration and use of the income of all funds arising from the sale or lease of the sixteenth section of land. This act also provided for the election of a township commissioner and three school trustees. When the funds were sufficient these trustees established a school, employed the teacher, and performed other duties in connection with the school affairs. The act of 1843 provided further for an elective and ex-officio board of county school commissioners who were to be in general charge of the school funds of the county.

There were no county superintendents nor examiners for teachers in the county at that time. However, we had what was known as the circuit superintendent whose jurisdiction of schools covered the same territory as that comprised by the circuit judge. He tried to visit all the schools in his circuit at least once each year. It was his duty to issue certificates to teachers. The applicants were not put to a written examination, as they are today. They were simply asked to answer a few questions orally. These were rarely asked by the circuit superintendent, but were propounded by one or more teachers appointed by him to conduct the examination. The superintendent sat back as a mere looker-on. W. H. Gillihan was the last circuit superintendent connected with this county and his term expired about 1874.

A short time afterwards, Prof. John Stackpole was appointed the first county superintendent of Izard County schools. Tom Evans was the next superintendent. From 1878 to 1919 county superintendents were done away with and instead there were county examiners. Both county superintendents and county examiners were at that time appointed by the courts. The county examiner conducted the examinations for teachers and also the county institutes. Accuracy in dates and arrangement in regular order cannot be given, but the following men have been county examiners of Izard County: H. C. Tipton, W. P. Moore, John H. Woods, J. W. C. Gardner, A. F. Benson, John F. Landers, J. D. Pane, Geo. W. Cypert, J. P. Bingham, W. M. Gentry, T. W. Simpson, T. H. Linn and Walter E. Schultz.

In 1874 the present state Constitution was adopted, which provided for a system of free schools to be supported by a tax of two mills, an annual per capita tax of one dollar, and a local district tax not to exceed five mills in any one year. This portion of the Constitution met with some fierce opposition in this county at the beginning, but after all, it was the foundation of the present school system. Tom Evans taught the first free school term in Izard County, at Lunenburg in the year 1875. The little log house stood about half a mile northeast of the place where the present building now stands.

As the public school system developed and as new educational demands and obligations came it was found that the local tax limits were inadequate. Hence the Legislature of 1905 submitted a constitutional amendment to be voted on in the 1906 general election, providing that the tax rate for the support of the public schools should be increased from two to three mills and that the maximum local tax rate should be increased to seven mills. Again in 1916 the maximum local district tax limit was raised by constitutional amendment to twelve mills. And again in the election of 1926 the people voted the raise to 18 mills. In this election Izard County voted two to one for the 18-mill limit. This was the best showing in any county in north Arkansas, which goes to show an increased interest in education in this county.

In 1920 the Legislature provided for the maintenance of a county board of education in each county of the state. The members of the board were elected by the people at the regular school election in May, one member being elected each time to serve a term of five years. This board had a number of duties and responsibilities in connection with the administration of the school affairs of the county, chief of these being the appointment of the county superintendent of schools. T. H. Linn had been elected to the office of the county superintendent by popular vote in 1919 for a term of two years. At the expiration of this term in 1921 he was appointed by the county board for a term of two years more, and was reappointed in 1923 for a term of three years. In 1926 he was succeeded by Karr Shannon who was appointed for a term of three years and then for another three years.

In 1932 the county board named O. A. Fulbright as superintendent for a term of three years. But the Legislature of 1933 abolished the office of county superintendent, along with the county board, and restored the county examiner with his selection to be made by the county judge on recommendation of the teachers of the county. Mr. Fulbright then became county examiner and served until 1937 when he was succeeded by Tom Simpson. The Legislature of 1941 created the office of county supervisor to be elected by a county board of five members. The newly elected board named Mr. Simpson as the county's supervisor, which office he still holds. The present county board is composed of John Williamson, A. J. Younger, Homer Harber, U. E. Hudson and R. L. Blair.

The county at one time had as high as 92 districts. But through a program of consolidation which got under way in 1930 the number of districts has now been reduced to 36.

There are five four-year high schools in the county, as follows: Melbourne, Calico Rock, Mt. Pleasant, Violet Hill and Oxford. The first two received the "B" rating this year; each of the last three was rated "C." Agriculture and home economics are taught at Melbourne, Calico Rock and Violet Hill, and Mt. Pleasant has extra buildings for these departments which are planned to be added in the near future. Each of the five high schools has a good gymnasium.

Some of the many other teachers prominent in school

HISTORY OF IZARD COUNTY

affairs of the county during the past quarter-century are as follows: S. E. Wells, G. S. Butler, H. D. Webb, Sam Linn, Mr. and Mrs. Dale Woods, Mrs. Clyde LaFevers, Mr. and Mrs. N. P. Ford, Mr. and Mrs. W. W. Haynes, Mrs. Velma Cypert Johnson, Mrs. Lela Evans Davis, Mr. and Mrs. Claude Caldwell, Ray E. Davis, Gulley Davis, Lee Evans, Herndon Frizzell, Rayburn O. Richardson, Mr. and Mrs. W. H. Jacobs, Catherine Ashley, Virgie Evans, Mr. and Mrs. Byron Jeffery, Ray Clark, Mrs. Nola Moody, Erlene Helm, S. W. Smith, W. O. Smith, Hattie Croom, Esther Wood, Orbra Richardson, Owen Harvelle, J. T. Atkinson, Guy Wiley, A. N. Wood, J. T. Byram, J. D. Guthrie, Mrs. Tom Simpson, Nancy Duren, Emma Campbell, Lawrence Harber, Ray Hall, C. J. Perryman, Mrs. S. E. Wells, Mrs. O. A. Fulbright, Remmel Billingsley, Mrs. Mildred Billingsley Shell, Mr. and Mrs. O. L. Baker, Joe Ward, Mr. and Mrs. Festus Girkin, Mr. and Mrs. Powell Dixon, Mr. and Mrs. F. L. McConnell, Frank Ray, Arden Norton, Mrs. Gradon Bone, Roy Bone, Mrs. Ruby Hightower, Mrs. Lula Jett Smith, Mrs. John M. Cavender, C. G. Pool and Cuthbert Pool.

IZARD COUNTY BANKING

THE FIRST BANK in Izard County was organized at Melbourne, in August, 1896. The original capital was $5,000 and the entire stock was owned by C. W. Brown, B. E. Massey, Rudolph Brown and W. F. Eatman, all of Mountain Home, Baxter County. C. W. Brown was the first president and Stephen Brown was the first cashier. In 1897 all the bank stock was sold to Izard County people. In 1899 S. R. Hinkle was elected president and J. B. Baker, cashier. R. D. Harris was appointed assistant cashier. In 1905 Mr. Baker was elected president and R. D. Harris, cashier. Mr. Harris remained as cashier for about 31 years, the longest service in this capacity in the history of the institution.

The bank still occupies the same place on the west side of the square on which it was started. It occupied the same stone building until 1929 when it was destroyed by fire. The bank was set up in a room of the courthouse for about a year, until a new brick building was constructed.

The present board of directors is as follows: G. H. Miller, president; A. J. Younger, vice president; Mrs. Borden Pearson, R. L. Blair and E. B. Watts. Mr. Blair was cashier for 13 years. During about two years of World War II the bank's personnel was made up entirely of women. Mrs. Pearson was cashier, Mrs. Opal Smith, assistant cashier, and Miss Mary Byram, clerk.

The present capital is $15,000, surplus is $15,000, and deposits total about $865,000.

HISTORY OF IZARD COUNTY

The Bank of Calico Rock was organized in 1903 with C. H. Hogan and O. S. Goodman as president and cashier, respectively. This bank was in operation until 1909 when it was succeeded by the Bluff City Bank. When the latter bank was organized, E. C. Parsons was elected president; Jeffery Dixon, vice president, and Asa M. Benbrook, cashier. The capital stock was $10,000.

The Peoples Bank of Calico Rock was organized in 1912 with S. E. McNeil as president; R. H. Wayland, vice president, and W. M. Gentry, cashier. The capital stock was $12,000.

The State Bank of Calico Rock, the present bank, was a merger of the Bluff City Bank and the Peoples Bank of Calico Rock, and began business May 1, 1914. The original capital stock was $25,000 and there was a surplus of $2,500. The officers elected were E. C. Parsons, president; R. H. Wayland, vice president, and E. C. Rodman, cashier.

The present officers are S. E. McNeill, president; Dr. Noel J. Copp, vice president; E. C. Rodman, cashier, and Roy Perryman and A. G. Perryman, assistant cashiers. The directors are McNeill, Copp, Rodman, Roy Perryman and L. E. Evans. The present capital stock is $25,000, surplus is $15,000, and deposits run approximately $1,600,000. The bank is not only the largest in the county, but one of the largest in north Arkansas.

The Bank of Franklin was organized in 1904 with a capital of $10,000. The first officers were Hodge Case, president; A. F. Batterton, vice president, and T. W. Simpson, cashier. Mr. Simpson later served as president, and was serving in this capacity at the time he was killed in a tornado which struck Franklin May 13, 1933. G. Gleghorn, E. G. Shell, W. J. Billingsley, W. E. Billingsley and Tom Simpson have served as cashier. The present cashier is R. M. Standerford, who has served since December, 1934, except for six months in 1945 when he worked with the State Banking Department. W. A. Gaston is president, and J. W. Cooksey, vice president. Other members of the board are J. S. Box, Mr. Standerford and Mrs. Sallie M. Simpson. The present capital is $10,000, with $10,000 surplus and about $260,000 in deposits.

The Bank of Franklin was probably at one time the only bank in the United States open for business. It happened during the "bank holiday" at the beginning of President Roosevelt's administration in 1933. There being no phone connections with Franklin, T. W. Simpson, cashier at the time, did not get a wire about the nation-wide bank closure. By the time he received the telegram through the mail the "holiday" had expired, and the bank never did close.

The Bank of Barren Fork was chartered at Mt. Pleasant October 30, 1913. The first board of directors was Dr. L. T. Evans, president; S. P. Thompson, vice president; A. L. Convers, W. K. McSpadden and A. J. Younger. S. M. McSpadden was cashier. The bank was opened for business in a rented room of the C. A. Evans drug store building, and was not moved to a building constructed for the purpose until October, 1915. A. J. Younger served as cashier for many years and was serving at the time the bank was voluntarily liquidated August 1, 1938. Depositors and stockholders were paid in full. The capital stock was $10,000.

The Bank of Oxford was open for business October 1, 1919, with Dr. J. H. Smith, president; A. H. Caldwell, vice president, and D. F. Croom, cashier. The capital stock was $10,000. W. M. Ford later became president. The bank closed for liquidation December 19, 1931, and liquidation was completed January 1, 1934. Depositors were paid in full.

The Izard County Bank, at Guion, was organized by J. W. Williamson in 1911 with Mr. Williamson as president and E. L. Collier as cashier. The stone bank building was all but completely destroyed when a tornado hit the town in April, 1929. But the bank rebuilt and continued in operation until November 17, 1930, when it was closed for liquidation which was completed November 28, 1933.

Thus there have been nine different banks in Izard County, covering a period of over a half-century. Only three of these banks are now in operation, but the county's banking history has been commendable due to the fact that no depositor has ever lost a penny through any closure.

IZARD COUNTY NEWSPAPERS

IZARD COUNTY has seen the establishment of several newspapers, but all of them except two have suspended publication. The first paper to make its appearance in the county was the *LaCrosse Post,* which was established at LaCrosse sometime in 1873 by James H. Graham, who published it until 1876 when he moved to Melbourne and started the *Melbourne Clipper.* This paper continued circulation until 1881. The year the *Clipper* suspended Buckley & Culp established the *Izard County Register* and ran it until 1887 when the paper was taken over by Dave Craige, who continued to run it until his death in 1907.

In 1883 K. W. C. Haun and G. W. Seay started the *Newburg Magnet,* which they published a few months at Newburg and then moved to Oxford where the name of the paper was changed to the *New Magnet* and published there about two years. In 1885 Haun came to Melbourne and established *The Tidings,* which he ran about a month and then leased it to C. C. Baker. A month later Baker leased it to J. N. Hutchinson. Soon afterward it suspended publication.

The *Franklin Item* was started at Franklin by Wm. H. V. Wahlquist in 1880 but folded up after a few months. The *Franklin Tidings* was the name of another paper established at that place, but the actual date or duration could not be ascertained.

The *Wheel,* an organ of the Wheel Association once

HISTORY OF IZARD COUNTY

active in the county, made its appearance at Newburg in 1886, with J. M. Elzey as editor, but it lasted only a year.

The *Izard County Democrat* was started in Melbourne by George Trevathan in 1891. He continued its publication a few years and then went to Batesville where he published the *Batesville Guard*.

The *Calico Rocket* was the first paper ever published at Calico Rock. It was started in 1903 by L. T. Frazier who published it but a short time. On August 18, 1904, the *Rocket* was taken over by the Bank of Calico Rock and edited by H. B. Dallan, who changed the name to *Calico Rock Progress*. The bank owned the paper until 1906, during which ownership there were four different ones employed as editors. In 1906 Dallan bought the paper and edited it until 1912 when it was sold to the present editor, Neill Brooks. During World War I Mr. Brooks served in the army from June 15, 1918, to May 5, 1919, and during the time the paper was put out by Misses Agnes and Annie Guthrie.

On January 1, 1930, Mr. Brooks sold the *Progress* to S. W. Taylor, who, with S. A. McCullough as partner, ran the paper for a few months. Then Mr. McCullough and Sylvester Smith bought from Taylor. A short time later, McCullough sold his interest to Ralph Combs. Smith and Combs published the paper until the early part of 1933 when J. B. Story bought it. Mr. Brooks bought the paper back January 15, 1934, after he had operated a newspaper at Heber Springs for several months. The paper is still edited and published by Brooks and, in addition to being active in civic affairs, he does a big business in job printing.

Mr. McCullough started the *Ozark Times* at Calico Rock in October, 1932, and published it continuously until June, 1937, when the paper suspended. He printed the paper on a news press that he had built himself. The press was operated by hand, and was such unique mechanism that it was widely publicized by other newspapers including the *Arkansas Gazette*. Mr. McCullough made a miniature pattern of the press and placed it on display once at a meeting of the Arkansas Press Association in Little Rock.

The *Guion Banner* was started at Guion in 1909 by H. C. Brooks, brother of Neill Brooks, but the paper was discontinued about a year later.

The next paper established at Melbourne was the *Melbourne Times*. It made its first appearance in 1896 on a handkerchief-size sheet published in a room of the old courthouse by Henry Trevathan. He continued to publish the paper for a few years and then sold to Lackey & Robinson. The paper finally got into the hands of R. J. Estes, about 1905, who published it until September, 1922, when he sold to E. A. Smith. Mr. Estes got his first experience in the newspaper business as helper in the office of the *Izard County Register*, starting at an early age.

Mr. Smith published the paper until November, 1932, when it was bought by Karr Shannon. He ran it until December, 1944, when he moved to Little Rock to take a job as columnist on the *Arkansas Democrat*. Shannon sold the paper to C. L. ("Bill") Coger in January, 1945. Coger, an experienced newspaperman who had previously edited papers at Hardy and Heber Springs and had spent about three years as employe on the *Times* under Shannon's ownership, has made some striking improvements on the paper, increasing both the size and circulation. He still gets out the paper every week and, in addition, finds time to be mayor of the town and direct a band for the Melbourne High School.

A 36-page edition of the *Times* published June 21, 1940, was the largest single issue of a newspaper ever published in the county and was said to be the largest hand-set weekly newspaper ever published in the state. However, four pages of the 36 were put out at the *Calico Rock Progress* plant.

This completes the history of newspapers in the county, except for a few school and church papers published at intervals.

MELBOURNE, PRESENT COUNTY SEAT

THE COUNTY SEAT was moved from Mt. Olive to Melbourne on May 10, 1875. The new location was about 15 miles east of the former town near the center of the county, and has remained here ever since.

The town of Melbourne was first known as Mill Creek and the post office was about a mile east of the present town. At this writing the old Mill Creek post office building is still standing and was used as a dwelling until recently. The town was named "Melbourne" by W. C. Dixon, and was laid off by James A. Claiborne, county surveyor at that time.

A large barn was used as a courthouse until 1878 when a frame structure was erected. The building site, on which the present building also stands, was secured from Tommy Richardson. He had raised a fine patch of turnips on the ground the previous year.

This first house stood until the morning of April 11, 1889, when it was destroyed by fire, and with it all the records and documents from the foundation of the county were consumed. The population of the town was about 300 at the time.

Before building again, a number of people wanted to move the county seat to some other part of the county. But appropriations were soon made to rebuild the house on the same spot of ground and E. C. Parsons, Elbert Benbrook and T. P. Powell were appointed commissioners to let the con-

First courthouse built at Melbourne.

HISTORY OF IZARD COUNTY

tract and superintend the building. The final report of the commissioners as to the building of the house was made August 9, 1890. This house was also a large frame structure and was little improvement over the other one. It was used for all business connected with court affairs and was also a kind of county and community center for other important occasions and entertainment.

But let us back up and get more of the early history of the town. The Mill Creek post office was established January 14, 1854, with William Sublett as postmaster. The office was discontinued July 9, 1866, and then re-established July 29, 1867, with John B. Dixon as postmaster. The name of the post office was changed to Melbourne February 16, 1876.

The Baptists established the first church here in 1848. A Union church was built in 1853. A Methodist church building was not constructed until 1879. A Presbyterian church house was erected in 1890 and stood until 1923 when it was made into a dwelling.

In 1870 the first schoolhouse was built. It stood south of the creek just east of the Powell grove. A combination hotel and boarding house was erected above the Powell spring. The town had a good boarding school for that time, and has been considered a good school center ever since.

The house across the creek was abandoned in 1896 and the school entered a new building just east of the present house. This building burned in 1904 and was soon replaced by another frame building. The last building remained until 1929 when the present tile building was erected. Since then, there have been four additional buildings on the campus—a gymnasium, agriculture building, home economics cottage, and building for grade classes.

The business district of Melbourne has suffered losses from four fires. In 1905 the north half of the west side of

The county's courthouse, completed in 1914, and burned in 1937.

the public square burned out, leaving only the bank building and the present theater building, which at that time was used as a store. The entire north and east sides, including the hotel, were burned out in 1908. Then, in 1911, the south side of the square went up in flames, including the printing plant and a large stock barn.

In 1929 a fire swept out all the business houses on the west side except the theater building and Byram's store.

The town suffered from a tornado in 1883 which leveled several buildings and killed three people.

Izard County's second courthouse stood until 1912 when it was torn away to give place to a large brick building. The new building was brought to completion in 1914, and was considered one of the finest in the state. It cost about $50,000 and was built under the administration of Judge

HISTORY OF IZARD COUNTY

P. C. Sherill. The commissioners were W. A. Wilson and J. W. Williamson, and the architect was Clyde A. Ferrell.

The tons of brick, cement and other building materials and furnishings were hauled by wagon-and-team from the railroad at Guion up Rocky Bayou Creek. The distance was 12 miles and the road was a makeshift, consisting of sand-beds, ruts and hills—and crossing the creek many times. This was the chief transportation avenue connecting the county seat with the railroad for about a quarter of a century before the Batesville-Mammoth Spring highway was completed through Melbourne in 1925.

On Sunday morning, December 5, 1937, the magnificent brick structure burned. The fire broke out in the attic near the dome of the huge clock which had been striking the time and rippling the waves of the ether with its beautiful tone for a radius of three or four miles for 23 years. Most of the records and valuable documents were saved. What were not moved out were preserved in the two fireproof vaults of the building.

County offices were moved into the Powell dwelling, a frame structure, on the southeast corner of the public square, and court was held in the new Baptist church, a stone building, about a block northwest until the building could be replaced.

The present fireproof courthouse was dedicated June 13, 1940, at a gala event attended by several state and national celebrities and some 3,000 spectators. The structure is said to have cost $150,000, part paid by the county and the balance by the Federal government through an N. Y. A. project. Erhart and Eichenbaum of Little Rock were the architects.

The building was started during the administration of Judge John W. Hammett, who was defeated by C. C. Aylor in 1938. Mr. Aylor took office January 1, 1939. Judge Ham-

Izard County's present courthouse.

mett had appointed the following commissioners: E. B. Watts, R. L. Blair, C. W. Gaston, W. W. Fudge and J. W. Webb. A plaque containing the list of commissioners was placed near the foundation on the northwest corner of the building. Also, Judge Hammett's name appears on the plaque. Judge Aylor retained as his commissioners only Mr. Watts and Mr. Blair, and when the building was completed an additional plaque was placed just inside of the north entrance containing the names of Judge Aylor and the two commissioners.

The Melbourne Resident N. Y. A. project, which built the courthouse, was the largest N. Y. A. project in the United States at the time. A camp a mile north of town covered several acres and had a dozen or more buildings most of which were stone veneer. About 150 boys were kept at the camp and trained in carpentry, masonry and other manual trades, each being worked a certain number of hours weekly on the courthouse building. It was a very expansive and expensive project in which the U. S. Government probably invested a million dollars or more. A few months after the courthouse was completed, the camp was abandoned and about the only signs left are the concrete foundations and stone walls of the buildings. The land was leased to the N. Y. A. by the late John C. Ashley.

A few years after the courthouse was completed in 1890 a fireproof stone building was erected on the courtyard south of the house to be used for the clerk's office and safe storage of records. This building was used by the county until the first brick courthouse came into use in 1914. After that, it was first rented as a law office to Bledsoe & Ashley. Later it was used as the office of Dr. W. S. Baldwin, physician and surgeon. About 1920, it was rented to the *Melbourne Times* which occupied the building until 1939 when the *Times* moved to other quarters so the N. Y. A. could dismantle the building.

Melbourne was a good business town almost from its foundation. While it never did go in strong for manufacturing, it was surrounded by a good farming section. It has had a cotton gin as far back as the 70's. A treadmill gin was once operated where Miller's store now stands. The machinery was propelled by a huge wheel caused to revolve by the weight of cattle treading on the periphery. The town once had a flour mill, and in the long, long ago operated a wagon and furniture factory. Lumber and stave mills have been located in or near the town at intervals. Transportation facilities and convenience of mail service were a constant drawback until the coming of automobiles and highways.

Today Melbourne has good schools, creditable business establishments, a bank and one of the best weekly newspapers in north Arkansas. It has had electric service for 17 years and, at the time this book goes to press, the town is installing a modern water system. The Baptist, Methodist and church of Christ each have good church buildings and regular services. There are also alert Masonic and veteran organizations. Recently a cold-storage plant was built, and the town has enjoyed a building boom of dwellings and business houses the past several years. R. O. Tomlinson is postmaster and C. L. Coger is mayor. The town is now a city of the second class.

CALICO ROCK, LARGEST TOWN

CALICO ROCK, Izard County's largest town and one of the leading business centers in north Arkansas, got its name from the broad stripes of assorted colors which nature painted on the face of the high perpendicular cliffs just below the town giving it the appearance of a huge piece of calico cloth.

The town is one of the oldest settlements on White River, but did not get a post office until August 23, 1851, when James Jeffery, a pioneer resident, was appointed the first postmaster. The post office was discontinued November 18, 1852, and was not re-established until May 2, 1879, when William M. Aikin was appointed postmaster. Previous to that time the area was thinly settled. Bartley Kennedy started a store there in 1857, and in 1859 Matthews and Burton (Capt. R. C. Matthews) opened a store. But they both closed out when the Civil War started.

Shortly after the re-establishment of the post office, Roby & Calloway opened a drug store and Kerr & Galloway put in a drygoods store. About a year later a large general store was added by W. E. Maxfield of Batesville, and operated by Charles R. Aikin.

When the first post office was established, mail was brought up from Batesville once a week. When the settlement began to take on the appearance of a town in the early 80's most of the goods came up the river on flatboats from New Orleans. Later, steamboats supplanted the flatboats.

Cotton was shipped down the river on boats, and timber was floated down in rafts.

John Q. Wolf of Batesville said that when his mother moved to the settlement in 1874 only one family lived there. Several families soon began moving in, he said, in order to have access to a good school being taught at Spring Creek, three and a half miles inland, by Dr. J. A. Kerr. A schoolhouse was not built at Calico Rock proper until about 1903. The first house was a one-room boxed affair, 30 by 40 feet.

Just as the town was taking on some size, a fire wiped out all the stores in 1897 or '98. On March 10, 1902, J. T. Garner began building the first new store since the fire. On the same day work of throwing up the grade for the railroad started. With the building of the railroad the town started a new growth. It became headquarters for the construction crews, and business went on a boom.

With the completion of the railroad the town took on a more rapid growth. Dozens of families built good homes. A business section came into existence with good mercantile establishments, cotton and produce markets, and everything that goes to make an ideal town, including newspaper and banks (treated in other chapters of this volume). About 1920 the town built a two-story grade and high school building. It was constructed of concrete blocks and was the finest in the county at the time. It is still in use, other buildings have been added, and at present a $20,000 school building program is in progress.

The town continued to grow until April 7, 1923, when sparks from a locomotive set fire to a warehouse near the sidetracks. A strong wind carried the fire through the business section. All stores on the east side of Main Street were burned out. Also, a block of buildings on the west side burned. In all, 28 buildings went up in smoke. The loss was approximately $75,000, which was largely replaced by the railroad and insurance companies. The business section was rebuilt with brick and stone structures.

The lower part of town in which a part of the business section is located has suffered three major floods. Most of the residential area is elevated and beyond reach of flood waters.

Today the town, a city of the second class, has a good school center, active churches and civic clubs, lumber mills, cotton gin, stave mill, market for all kinds of timber and farm products, large mercantile establishments on both sides of the bayou, one of the largest banks in north Arkansas, a modern printing plant and good newspaper. It was the first town in the county to have an electric light and power system, and put in a municipal water system several years ago. It is served by two state highways, Nos. 5 and 56, and is within 15 miles of the Norfork dam and lake, the coming resort area of the Southland. The present population is approximately 1,000. Tom Kerr is the present mayor and E. T. Estes is postmaster.

OTHER TOWNS

BATTLES

THE PLACE now known as Battles was first called Hamm after A. J. Hamm, who was postmaster from 1893 to 1906, when the office was discontinued. The office was re-established May 13, 1907, with the name of "Battles" after F. M. Battles. Phillip D. Parish was the first postmaster under the new name. F. M. Battles became postmaster in 1910. The office was moved one and one-half miles west of the present location in 1922. Mrs. Willie Dover is now postmaster.

BOSWELL

At one time the town was called Wideman, the depot was called Boswell and the post office was Cook. The first office at this place was Wideman, but was soon discontinued because the county already had a "Wideman." The office was established as "Cook" April 5, 1906, with Meredith Little as the first postmaster. It was named after John Cook. It was changed to "Boswell" September 4, 1915, with Mrs. Rosa B. Flemming as postmaster. It takes its present name from Robert Boswell. A. T. Smith is now the postmaster.

BROCKWELL

Brockwell is the youngest town in the county, the post office having been established here February 1, 1926, one year after the completion of the Batesville-Mammoth Spring highway. Homer E. Jennings was the first postmaster. The place was named after George Brockwell, who operated a store here and owned the 40 acres of ground on which the town was built.

This place maintains a new community hall, completed in 1947, which is a convenient gathering place for singings, speakings and revival meetings. The town stands at the intersection of highways 9 and 56. Mrs. Ethel Brockwell, daughter-in-law of the man from which the town took its name, is postmaster.

CRESWELL

Among the early settlers who came to this county were the Creswells. They settled on White River about two miles south of Calico Rock. A post office was not established at this place until May 5, 1902. The office took its name from its first postmaster, Cyrus J. Creswell. S. E. McNeill, now of Calico Rock, served as postmaster about 35 years. The present postmaster is Mrs. Lela F. Russell.

CROKER

The railroad station at this place has been called "Croker Spur" since about 1904, the name probably being the fruit of inspiration from the "croak" of the big bullfrogs common along the river. The post office was established August 11, 1924, with O. D. Pence as first postmaster. The office took the exact name of the station. It was changed to "Croker" November 1, 1933, while E. C. Roberts was postmaster. It still goes by that name. Mrs. Rachel Maria Hume is postmaster at present.

CROSS ROADS

A settlement was started in the present Cross Roads vicinity shortly after the Civil War, and the place took its name from the fact that the Old Military Road and the Jacksonport

Road crossed here. The Military road ran east and west and the Jacksonport road north and south. A post office was established here March 28, 1911, with James T. Dockins as the first postmaster.

The office was discontinued in 1940, but was re-established about a year later. Mrs. Cora Jennings is now the postmaster.

Day

The Day post office was first established some time in the year 1890, with Mrs. Vina Montgomery as postmaster. After several years the office was discontinued. It was established the last time February 25, 1893, with Nancy M. Montgomery as postmaster. The place was named after Postmaster General Day who was in charge of the Department at Washington at the time the office was established. Arch Gleghorn is now postmaster.

Dolph

The Dolph post office and schoolhouse are probably farther away from the county seat than any other place in the county. The present post office at Dolph was established May 3, 1911, with Ernest Regelman as postmaster. It was not learned why the place was so named. Sanford Wayland is postmaster.

Forty-Four

A number of reports have been given as to just why this place is so named. However, there have been no grounds to believe it has any relation to a rifle. One of the most authentic reports is that it was so named because 44 names were submitted to the Department previous to the time the office was established August 28, 1928. John W. Key was the first postmaster. Coy Richardson is the present postmaster.

HISTORY OF IZARD COUNTY

Franklin

Franklin is one of the oldest towns in the county, the post office having been established here as early as October 7, 1848. Levi Bowling was the first postmaster. At that time the territory was a part of Fulton County and remained so until October, 1875, when it was changed to Izard.

Like LaCrosse, this place was first settled by the Watkinses. They came here from Franklin, Tennessee. Soon after they settled in this section they sought the establishment of two post offices, one near the present site of LaCrosse and the other near what is now Franklin. There were many wild haws in the Franklin country and they submitted that name for the upper office and "Franklin" for the lower. The U. S. Post Office Department got the names reversed in some manner, and the former was named Franklin and the latter Wild Haws.

The town has maintained a good school for many years, operating a Smith-Hughes department several years, and it is now a part of one of the largest consolidated districts in the state.

A tornado hit the town in the spring of 1933 and destroyed most of the business section and many of the dwellings, which have been rebuilt. Three persons were killed.

The town is situated in one of the best farm sections of the county, being near Strawberry River. It was one of the first towns to operate a cotton gin and flour mill.

Several years ago Franklin was incorporated and a large community hall built. D. F. Bryant is the present mayor, and Mrs. Glenn Roberts is postmaster.

Gid

The Gid post office was named after "Uncle Gid" Bruce, who happened to step in to warm while a group of men were sitting around the stove arguing over a name for a post office, in the store of John Hanna on a cold, wintry day. The office was established March 23, 1888, and Mr. Hanna was appointed the first postmaster. E. E. Reid is the present postmaster.

At about the same time an office was established two miles south of Lunenburg, known as "Adler," named after Nathan Adler, pioneer merchant of Batesville. J. L. Byler was made the first postmaster. Later, J. M. Gilbert became postmaster and held the office until 1909 when it was discontinued.

Gorby

Gorby is one of the late post offices in the county. It was established August 15, 1923, with Homer E. Jennings as postmaster. Previous to that time it was called "Engle." It could not be learned just why the place was so named. The present postmaster is Mrs. Audie P. Mason.

Guion

Wild Haws Landing near the present town of Guion was one of the earliest settlements in the county. The landing was discontinued about the time the White River railroad was built in 1902 and the railroad station was known as "Yancy." A post office was established some time in the 90's known as "Louis," but was short lived. The railroad station and post office became known as "Guion" April 24, 1903, and Joseph L. Byler was appointed first postmaster. The town was named after J. H. Guion, who had official connection with the railroad company at that time.

For many years Guion was one of the busiest towns in the county, being a freight outlet to Melbourne and surrounding towns, and it continued as such until after the completion of the Batesville-Mammoth Spring highway.

In the early part of the century one of the largest stave

mills in the White River country was operated here for several years. The Guion Silica Company operates a sand plant here, one of the largest in the state, and is the chief source of employment for the town. Mrs. Mertie Harris of Little Rock is general manager. Also a marble quarry is operated south of town.

The town has been incorporated for many years, and was the first town in the county to install a water system. Arch Smith is the present mayor and Walter Hayden is postmaster.

Guion has probably suffered more disasters than any other town in the state, having been flooded four or five times and completely wiped out by a tornado in the spring of 1929.

IUKA

A post office was established at Iuka, Baxter County, July 26, 1876, with Thomas J. Wayland as postmaster. The office was located in Izard County after December 8, 1887. It could not be learned why the place was so named. Irshell Russell is the present postmaster.

The Iuka school district is divided between Izard and Baxter counties.

JUMBO

The Jumbo post office was established April 21, 1891, with Ambros C. Jeffery as the first postmaster, according to records from Washington. There were no elephants down there; the settlement is mostly Democratic. It is said the folk attempted to name the post office after "Jimbo" Smith, but the Post Office Department read it wrong and wrote it "Jumbo." Mrs. Marvin Hunt is the present postmaster.

KNOB CREEK

This place was first known as "Byler." A post office by

that name was established there June 15, 1889, the place taking its name from the first postmaster, David J. Byler. It was changed to Knob Creek February 24, 1913, with Robert L. Clem as postmaster. It was named for the creek which runs through the settlement. The creek takes its name from Pilot Knob near by. Frank Page is now the postmaster.

LaCrosse

The first inland post office in Izard County was established at Wild Haws January 20, 1848, with James D. Watkins as postmaster. The building in which this office was housed still stands about two miles east of the present town of LaCrosse, and is used as a tenant house on the W. W. Fudge farm (old Dr. Watkins plantation).

The name of the office was changed to LaCrosse December 6, 1869, when S. H. Wren was postmaster. Shortly after the Civil War, two railroad companies made surveys for prospective roads which intersected at the site of the present town. It was thought at the time that both roads would be built, and thus the name. The Larkin-Franklin road and the road connecting Violet Hill with Highway 69 cross here.

The early history of LaCrosse as a school town is treated in another chapter.

Mrs. P. O. Wren is the present postmaster.

Lafferty

The post office here was first named Anderson, after Robert C. Anderson, the first postmaster. It was established August 23, 1882, and was discontinued January 31, 1931.

The Lafferty post office was established July 1, 1936, with Mrs. Edna M. Roberts as postmaster, who still holds the position. It was named for John Lafferty, the first settler.

Anderson was a boom town during World War I when

large-scale manganese mining was in operation in the vicinity. From about 1925-28 F. L. McConnel taught a one-year high school here, and Anderson and Williamson school districts were among the first to be consolidated. It was in this consolidated district that the first school bus in the county was operated.

LARKIN

Larkin is one of the oldest settlements in the county and was once known as Philadelphia. In 1870 J. W. C. Gardner established the North Arkansas Academy here in an old log schoolhouse that stood for some 20 years. The school was the chief interest of the small town and was at one time a leader in north Arkansas. The academy continued with little hindrance until 1905.

The Larkin post office was established October 6, 1894, with James L. Forrest as first postmaster. Hubert Jett is the present postmaster.

It is said, though not confirmed, that the office was named for Larkin Box who died at Violet Hill a few years ago.

The old Philadelphia church at this place is probably the oldest church house in the county, and one of the oldest in the state. It was built by donations in 1857, and has been kept in a fairly good state of repair since then. For years the old building was a kind of community and county center. The house is still used by all denominations, chiefly the Methodist and Baptist. For many years it has been the custom each first Sunday in July to have an all-day service and reunion of old citizens.

LUNENBURG

Lunenburg is an old settlement. It was a pretty fair town for several years before the Civil War, but a post office was not established there until February 3, 1868. Robert R. Case was the first postmaster. The office was discontinued May 12, 1868. Exactly two years later it was re-established with John Carney as postmaster. It was again discontinued November 8, 1872. It was re-established August 11, 1873, with Harvey R. Landers as postmaster. The office played out again April 9, 1883, but resumed permanent operation April 13, 1891, with William G. Cypert as postmaster.

When the post office was established the first time, the question of a name came up. There was already a general store in operation. The merchant, "Bob" Case, asked a group of loafers what to name the post office. An old German, who liked his "dram," was pretty well organized at the time, and probably seeing visions of his old home town left behind said: "Call her Lunenburg, by God!"

Mrs. Zelda Banning is the present postmaster.

A school building, with a lodge hall upstairs, was built shortly after the close of the Civil War and remained in use for school purposes until a few years ago when the district built a new stone building. The old school building is now used as a church house by the Baptists. The school bell which is still in use is said to be the first bell ever brought to the county.

The Rocky Bayou Baptist Association, still active and growing over a large area, had its birth here over 100 years ago.

Mt. Pleasant

This place was first called Barren Fork and a post office was established by that name May 25, 1876. Milton L. Shaver was the first postmaster. According to R. M. Thompson, that part of the county was actually pretty barren at the time. A fork of Polk Bayou was a mile to the east, and a fork of Lafferty Creek was about two and one-half miles to the west.

HISTORY OF IZARD COUNTY

The town was also nicknamed "Dry Town," an appellation with no Eighteenth Amendment significance, said Mr. Thompson, but it was so called because only a few wells were dug by the early settlers, who depended entirely upon cisterns for their water.

Young ladies sometimes change the destinies of towns as well as of men—and that's what happened to Barren Fork. When Miss M. E. Moore went to Jackson, Mississippi, to attend school, the students asked her if the place where she lived was really barren. When she came home, she had her father, O. P. Moore, a prominent man there, to circulate a petition for a change of name. The post office was changed to its present name October 29, 1914, and Helen R. Bone was the first to serve as postmaster under the new name. A. L. McSpadden is the present postmaster.

This place has a wide reputation as a school town, and was one of the old academy towns of the state. Near the close of the last century people came here from many parts of the state for school purposes. Many of them boarded. It now has one of the most beautiful high school buildings in north Arkansas.

Mt. Pleasant also has the distinction of being the only town in the county ever to maintain a hospital. The town is strongly Presbyterian. In 1928 the Woman's Board of the Presbyterian Church, U. S. A., with some donations from the community, built and equipped a modern hospital here. It had a wide patronage and operated until 1941 when it was discontinued. The school district bought the building and the furnishings were moved to a Presbyterian health center at Cotton Plant.

A gymnasium and community hall was erected near the school plant in 1931 with community donations and a grant from the Board of National Missions of the Presbyterian

HISTORY OF IZARD COUNTY

Church, U. S. A., and is operated by the church for the benefit of the community and school.

Mt. Olive

The present town-site of Mt. Olive is probably the oldest in the county. The first post office in the county was established here December 27, 1831. At that time the place was called "Pine Bayou" and the post office went by that name. John A. Allen was the first postmaster. The county seat of Izard County was moved here from old Athens in 1836 and remained here until May 10, 1875, when it was permanently established at Melbourne.

The town was changed to "New Athens" January 29, 1842, with Asa M. Fitch as the first postmaster under the new name. On January 4, 1847, the name of the town and post office was changed to "Mt. Olive," the name being taken from the hill east of the town.

Mrs. Pearl Dixon is the present postmaster and has held the position since 1922.

Myron

The post office at Myron was established April 18, 1904. Wm. A. Jackson was appointed first postmaster. He held the position until the first of 1940 when he retired. The office was named after a Senator Myron who died about the time the office was established. Leonard Ferguson is now postmaster.

Newburg

Newburg was formerly known as Newburgh, and a post office was established by that name March 31, 1868, with Allen Gilbert as first postmaster. The name was changed to Newburg March 23, 1892. The place has always had good churches and a good rural school. It was at one time one of the thriving business towns of the county, and boasted a good lumber mill.

Until about 20 years ago, Newburg was one of the major political precincts in the county. That was before territory was cut off in the formation of the Brockwell and Bandmill precincts.

Mrs. Glenna L. Cone is present postmaster of the town.

Oxford

The town of Oxford was one time called "Crooms Mill" and a post office was established by that name August 8, 1878, with James H. McCullough as postmaster. It continued under this name until March 24, 1882, when Emory S. Pearson was appointed postmaster. He immediately had the name changed to Oxford. No one seems to know why the name was changed unless it was for convenience.

About two years ago the town was incorporated, and in 1947 established a telephone system with long-distance connections. Uen Benbrook is the present mayor.

Oxford has always been known as a good school town, and was one of the early high school centers of the county. During recent years it has won state renown in basketball.

Gradon Bone is the present postmaster.

Pineville

Pineville was named from the many pines surrounding the settlement. The post office was established April 22, 1867, with James B. Roe as postmaster. The office was discontinued April 30, 1915. It was re-established as "Whit" May 24, 1920, with Young Whitfield as postmaster. It was again changed to Pineville April 17, 1922. Phillip Wayland is now the postmaster.

One of the earliest cotton gins in this section was established here.

Sage

The Sage post office was established August 11, 1887, with Dr. John W. Byler as first postmaster. The office was first located at the "Felts place" about a mile southeast of the present location. The office was moved to the present town in 1909 when P. J. Puckett was appointed postmaster. The place is said to have been named for the tall sage grass that once grew so easily in the vicinity. Harry Clark is now postmaster.

Stella

Stella was established with a post office December 27, 1894. James H. Bone was the first postmaster. Data was not available as to the reason the place was so named, but it is said that it was named after the daughter of one of the town's citizens at the time the post office was established. Mrs. Dewey Reeves is now postmaster.

This post office had its largest volume of business back in the latter part of the 1930's when a C. C. C. camp was located about a mile north.

Sylamore

Sylamore was named after Sylamore Creek, which ran into White River on the Stone County side. The creek was named after an old Indian horse thief, called "Chief Sylamore." For months the white settlers tried to blot him out. Finally he was shot and fell into the creek near where the bridge now hangs.

A post office was established in Stone County February 5, 1851, with Tobias S. Rudolph as postmaster. An office was established on the Izard County side of the river December

18, 1905, and called "East Sylamore." William W. Brooks was the first postmaster. The Stone County office was discontinued and the Izard County side became known as "Sylamore" on August 15, 1930.

John Williamson is the present postmaster, and is the oldest postmaster in service in the county.

Twin Creek

A post office was established at Twin Creek June 3, 1908, with Charles S. Brown as postmaster. The name is taken from two creeks that run into White River in the vicinity. Jeff Cooper is the present postmaster.

For many years the Twin Creek school district had two schoolhouses—one at the south extremity of the district and the other in the north part. This was not due to crowded conditions, but because the two settlements were several miles apart and separated by the poorest type of road.

Violet Hill

Mrs. Kirk Stephens named the place "Violet Hill" because of the many violets that grew on the hill that is today graced by one of the best high school buildings in the county. The post office was established July 12, 1858, with James McCuistion as postmaster. It was discontinued January 29, 1867, and was then re-established June 24, 1878, with James F. Barnes as postmaster. J. A. Billingsley took the office in 1893 and served continuously a total of 45 years until his death. He probably holds a state record, and likely few, if any, in the United States equal this record.

Since about 12 school districts were consolidated in 1930 Violet Hill has one of the largest high schools in the county. At the time of the consolidation it was the largest rural consolidated school in Arkansas, and was one of the pioneers in large-scale consolidations in both the county and state.

Mrs. Tressie Box is the present postmaster.

WIDEMAN

The post office at Wideman was established February 6. 1872, with David C. Shaver as first postmaster. At that time the town was located in Fulton County. It was changed into Izard County in 1874, and then discontinued April 3, 1886. It was re-established January 8, 1887, with James M. Kankey as postmaster. Marvin Webb is now postmaster.

WISEMAN

The town was named after a member of the Wiseman family who settled there in the early days. The post office was established April 10, 1901, with Monroe Montgomery as postmaster. The town now has a modern school building and operates one of the best rural schools in the county. The community is favorably located in the fertile valley of Strawberry River. Mrs. Neva Dillard is postmaster.

ZION

The town takes its name from the Zion Hill Baptist Church, one of the early churches of the county. A post office was established here June 17, 1886. William T. Campbell was the first postmaster. The territory around this place is in the nature of a plateau and well watered by small creeks.

In 1912-14 T. H. Linn taught a high school here and there were a number of boarding students. The town has always been a good trade center for the east part of the county. R. K. Fletcher is postmaster.

IZARD COUNTY AND WARS

WE APPRECIATE THE FACT that the history of Izard County does not have to deal with downfalls and uprisings of any vaunted civilization. This has never been a section of conflicts. The people have been intelligent, kind and hospitable. Scarcely any murders have been committed throughout the entire history of the county. It is enough for us to know that our forefathers were human beings—they lived and acted their parts, and all they did contributed to everything that now prevails. They were here first and did their work as human beings unmanacled by prejudice and disagreements. As men and women, they performed a life's work, died and were buried. They cleared farms, made roads, and enacted laws—all for their own comfort and well being, the highest aim in life. They seemed to assume the attitude that by the sweat of their brows should they live and that he who provided not for himself had denied the faith and was worse than a heathen. They labored to better their condition and ours. They were your fathers and mine.

It would be useless to go into detail here and tell about the cause of the Civil War. Nothing needs to be said about the conventions held in the South for the purpose of discussing the question of secession. Arkansas happened to be located in the Southland, and Izard County happened to be located in Arkansas. Negro slaves were needed in the hot fields, and, like other sections of the South, Izard County used its share of these people. There is no room here for discussing the question of slavery. As environment must have its course, the people of Izard County gave very little thought to the question of whether it was right or wrong to use negro slaves. The rest of the South used slaves, and Izard County used slaves.

At the approach of the Civil War, when the question of secession was being discussed, a majority of the people in Izard County were opposed to it. But when actual hostilities began, all but a very few were naturally in full sympathy with the Southern cause.

Several companies of soldiers were raised within the county for service in the Confederate Army. One, gathered by Captain Deason, served in the Seventh Arkansas Regiment. Four, commanded respectively by Capts. C. C. Elkins, T. N. Smith, Hugh A. Barnett and T. A. Mason, became a part of the Ninth Arkansas Regiment. Two, commanded respectively by Capts. C. Cook and Richard Powell, served in Colonel Freeman's regiment of cavalry. Three, commanded respectively by Capts. T. M. Gibson, R. C. Matthews and Samuel Taylor, formed a part of Colonel Shaler's regiment. Also a portion of the company was raised by Capt. John H. Dye, the other part being raised in Independence County. A part of another was raised by Capt. James Huddleston, the other part being recruited in what is now Sharp County. Some individuals went out and joined other companies being established for the Southern army.

At the beginning of the war there were several Union men in the county. They left the county and went to Rolla, Missouri, where they were organized into a company by Capt. L. D. Toney and served in the Federal army. Izard was very faithful to the cause. All the able-bodied men in the county and many boys under twenty years of age enlisted in the armies. Only the old, the feeble, and the invalids were left at home with the women and children.

HISTORY OF IZARD COUNTY

There was no fighting or bushwhacking among the citizens on Izard County soil, but the county was frequently overrun by scouting parties from the opposing forces and all stock and provisions carried away. This caused suffering among the citizens for food. It is said that parties of women, each accompanied by an old man, frequently hauled cotton inside the Union lines and exchanged it for salt and other necessities.

Conditions became so severe that meat had to be concealed from the scouting parties by hiding it in straw beds, under brush heaps, and in piles of rocks. Some saved their corn by shelling it and hiding it in the hollow walls of houses, between the weatherboarding and the inside-boarding. A hole at the bottom served the convenience of drawing out the grain as it was needed. Salt became a luxury. Many dug up the dirt in their smokehouses and boiled out the salt. Bed clothes and other garments were sometimes carried off by the scouting parties and burned in the woods.

But the destructive effects of war in Izard County were far short of what they were in a number of other sections of the South where actual battles were fought and hundreds in their youthful prime were shot down.

Izard County barely felt the effects of the Spanish-American War. But in World War I there were about 360 Izard County men in the army and navy, many of whom fought overseas. This was the cause of many tears and heartaches, but few of the boys from this county received severe wounds, and fewer appeared on the casualty list. The following lost their lives during the war:

Lt. Cecil C. Smith, Ullman Benbrook, Morrill B. Jackson, Manuel Thomason, Nealey May, Oscar Moore, Herbert S. Rowden, Troy Forrest, Lee Pentecost, Herman Hodges, Luther Clift, Henry Vannatter, Ernest Tomlinson, Vol Simpson, Herman Weaver, Osco Berry, George Kankey, Conrad Miller, Willie Warren and Silas Layton.

As in every section of the nation, World War II struck a horrible blow in Izard County. Approximately 1,300 of our boys were called to the ranks, serving in every branch of the armed service. Hundreds of them were in the thick of the fight, and scores were wounded or killed.

According to a printed release from the U. S. War Department in June, 1946, the following Izard County men lost their lives:

Pfc. Tovel O. Anold, Pvt. Lanceford H. Balch, Pvt. Duane Ball, Sgt. Thurston L. Beard, Pfc. Edmund Biles, Pvt. James H. Bone, Pvt. Cairel W. Birmingham, Pvt. Floyd E. Byler, Pfc. Lloyd A. Byler, Pfc. Olen Copeland, Pvt. Noble R. Craig, Pfc. Paul C. Dalrymple, Pfc. Aubrey W. Finley, Pfc. Fred Floyd, Second Lt. Robert L. Hengel, Second Lt. Gerold G. Hill, T/Sgt. James A. Frizzell, Pvt. Otis L. Ivie, Pfc. Elbert E. Jones, Pfc. Finis A. Kidwell, Pvt. Roy H. Killian, Pvt. Fred Lancaster, S/Sgt. Charles L. Martin, Pvt. Robert G. Miller, Pvt. Doyle C. Morgan, Pfc. Ewell W. Sanders, Pfc. Grover A. Sanders, Pvt. Talbert A. Marlin, T/5 Raymond F. Talburt, Pvt. Elmer J. Thomas, S/Sgt. Darwin D. Thompson, T/4 Ezra L. Vaughn, Pfc. Chester W. Vest, Pvt. Herbert Z. Ward, Pvt. Vernon G. Watkins, Pfc. Lawrence L. Wayland and Pvt. Charles H. Wilson.

A summary of war casualties in the U. S. Navy, released in 1946, lists the following from Izard County killed in action: Texas Thomas Kent, Jr., Seaman 2c (one of the first casualties, killed at Pearl Harbor); Rayford Dave Phillips, Seaman 2c; Wayne Scott Wilson, Aviation Ordnanceman 2c.

Since the close of the war most of the boys have returned home and many have taken up the same abode, finding Izard County a greater blessing after a view of other parts of the world. The fighting was done at sea and across the seas, but those who remained at home during the war keenly felt the effects in shortages of food and other needs. Izard County was loyal to the cause, going over the top in all Red Cross, U. S. O. and War Bond drives.

SINGINGS AND DANCES

MANY OF THE OLDSTERS remember when one of the chief entertainments of a community was the old-fashioned singing. These were usually held at some home where there was an organ. Everybody and his brother and sister would be there. Old and young would take part. The organist would usually play by chord. If there was no organ in the vicinity, they would go ahead and have singings anyway. There were always plenty of good singers, and a good leader and a tuning-fork were the only essentials to keep them going.

There were no radios in that day, but rural telephone lines reached into nearly every part of the county. Often the receiver was lifted off the hook and everybody on the party line not able to attend would listen in.

A singing was also a weekly event wherever there was a church or schoolhouse. It was held on Sunday afternoons or Sunday nights. Several communities still stick to this old tradition, and singing schools are yet pretty common over the county.

And you should get grandma and grandpa to tell you how they used to "swing 'em on the corner" at the old country dances. Up until a few decades ago square dances were staged in every community at least one night a week through the winter—usually every night of Christmas week. The dances were held in connection with weddings, house-raisings, hog-killings, wood-choppings and similar gatherings and community activities.

The dances were not sponsored in clubhouses, school buildings or other public places. There was always some farmer obliged to set the chairs around the wall, move the rest of the furniture out of the "livin' room" for a night and let everybody "swing 'em" by the warmth and light of the big fireplace and a kerosene lamp or two on the mantel.

"Partners for a quadrille," shouted the caller, causing the outside loafers to rush indiscriminately for favored positions from which to witness the hoedown. During the long continued tuning process of the fiddler, the dancers exchanged glances and grimaces, compliments and colloquy, and some of the gayer lads cut the "pigeon wing" and other didoes on the corners, to the infinite delight of the smirking Sallies.

Women in ginghams, cotton check and calico, and low-heeled shoes, and men in shirt-sleeves, duckin' and hobnails kept the squares going 'round and 'round from 9 p. m. till 2 or 3 in the morning. The lanky man in the corner with a voice like a steamboat whistle called:

> *Tighten up the bellybands and loosen up the traces;*
> *All join hands and get to your places.*

The dancers grabbed hands and formed a ring. The man in the corner began to sing:

> *Crack that whip, jerk the line;*
> *Let's all start dancing and have a good time.*

The fiddler would strike up *Turkey in the Straw*, or some other snappy tune, at a fast clip while the caller began jigging and chanting something of the following patter:

> *S'lute your partner and let her go;*
> *Balance all and do-se-do.*
> *Swing your gal and run away;*
> *Right and left the gents sashay.*

How they would swing 'em! Full skirts swirled. Everybody danced. The frame house swayed, the floor boards groaned, and the clapboards rattled. They could be heard a mile.

Square dance calling used to be considered "something you was born with." And callers had dozens of dance combinations to choose from, and any number of humorous chants. It was customary to set the dances in motion by singing something like

> *First gents out and swing Sally Goodin.*
> *Now your taw;*
> *The gal from Arkansaw!*
> *Then Sally Goodin*
> *And then your taw;*
> *Now don't forget your old grandmaw!*

The caller usually stood against the wall near the fiddler, and could give patented calls, or make up a few as he went along.

A fiddler didn't have to be a professional to take care of a country dance. There were good fiddlers a-plenty who could play "by ear," and cuss "by note" in case the dance turned into a row, as it sometimes did. If a fiddler could play at least two tunes well, he was good for an all-night dance.

While the old-time dances had their merits of fun, frolic and exercise, they had their pernicious points, too. Whiskey sometimes flowed all too freely outside the glow of the kerosene lamps—and fist-fights and loud profanity frequented the dark environment out in the yard. Neighborhood grudges many times clashed at dances. Saddle horses were unbridled and scared away. All this, along with other mischief and petit crimes, likely had much to do with the passing of the institutional square dance from the countryside. Township constables and deputy sheriffs were at times inadequate to cope with the situation. And country churches began to frown on dances. Anywhere there was a fiddle, preachers maintained, there was bound to be sin.

Since the close of the war dances have again sprung up in a town or two. But not the old-fashioned kind, and they are not held in private homes. The squares have been supplanted largely by twosomes and lively steps and jitter-bugging, in Legion huts or other convenient places, manipulated to the sound of a red-hot orchestra.

In Izard County today there may be an occasional home singing, or snap party, or sociable—there may even be a square dance at a farm home every now and then. But the general entertainment in this progressive county is far different from what it was back when "Uncle Milt" Oldfield waved the tuning fork for the host of singers, or when grandma and grandpa stamped the floor to the tune of Tonky Dixon's fiddle.

CHURCHES AND PREACHERS

THE CENSUS as early as 1850 listed for Izard County four Methodist church houses, three Baptist and two Presbyterian. A few years later a Christian church was organized. Today the leading churches in respect to membership are the Baptist, church of Christ, Methodist and Presbyterian.

It would be all but impossible to list the meeting houses in the county by church names. In some communities the various religious sects use the same building. In some of the other places, where there are no church buildings, the schoolhouses are often used for religious services. In at least six towns, one to three churches have regular preaching services, along with regular weekly meetings of young people's unions, Sunday School, Bible study and other auxiliary organizations.

Late summer is the time of year when the tranquil stillness of starlit nights is constantly interrupted by strong-lung evangelists coercing sinners to come to God. Since many of the meeting houses are small and poorly ventilated for hot weather, it is the usual procedure in rural areas to throw up a brush arbor in a shady nook at the fork of the creek, near a cool spring, or at some other convenient place in the vicinity.

These meetings are little digressive of the oldtime camp meetings when people came for 10 to 25 miles in wagons or on horseback and camped for a month or more, spending their time attending the sermons, praying and telling about various religious experiences, cooking and eating, playing games, and visiting with relatives and friends.

As a rule, these meetings call for two services each day—morning and night. But the night services are the more impressive and the better attended. Devil-chasers, like the oldtime Moody and Sunday and lesser lights, still stalk through the hill country and up the creeks, breathing danger of hell-fire from every pore. Imps and sin are driven from their lurking places, often with great shouting. The end of the world and the "second coming" are proclaimed daily. Youth of both sexes and many hard-hearted oldsters are stirred mightily, and to happy effect.

The duration of a series of meetings may run from two weeks to a month, depending upon the interest, weather conditions, and the suppply of country hams, barnyard fryers and garden vegetables.

Night services commonly begin about sundown and may last to 10 o'clock or midnight. The sermon itself may stretch through one to three hours, depending largely upon the larynx of the minister and the interest and patience of the congregation.

Back in the early days of the county's history the parents would bring their youngsters along and pallet them down on quilts around the outside of the arbor. Sometimes these quilts would cover a quarter-acre of ground. Buggies and hacks and wagons and saddled horses and mules would take up an acre or more.

There, under the canopy of the open sky, amid lamp bugs and horseflies and black gnats and singing mosquitoes, the babies would repose—sleep to the melody of song and hallelujahs and oratorical outbursts and shouts and amens. After the services there would be a rustle of skirts among the pallets, every mother trying to locate her baby.

As in yesteryear, the summer arbor meeting still serves as a kind of annual community affair—of benefit to all classes of people. It is a blessing to the saints, an opportunity for the sinner to get right with God, entertainment to many, and "somewhere to go" for everybody. Those who are immune to any interest or influence of the services, take to the dark outskirts of the meeting ground and tell yarns, spoon or swap horses.

The oldtime leather-lunged, hairy-chested preachers of the early days are not to be ridiculed or condemned. They played a great part in making the county a better place in which to live. To bring the practices of many of these conscientious servants into contempt, would be to condemn John the Baptist who, in the days of greatness, roared up Jordan valley in camel-skin raiment to the stern vexation of unbelievers. Many of these oldtimers were well educated and could have confounded the theological professors with their knowledge of the scripture. Most of them were sincere to the core, and got little more for their services than the fried chicken they consumed in the surroundings during the course of the meeting. With them, duty to God came first; money was secondary.

De E. Bradshaw of Omaha, Nebraska, a native Izardite, tells of the debates that were held in the early days between ministers of the Baptist and Christian churches, or between the ministers of the Methodist and one of the other denominations. "These debates were held on questions of faith, or mode of baptism by emersion or sprinkling, or on church government," Mr. Bradshaw said. "They were held in rural communities, usually in the summertime, and ran about three days. They began about 10 o'clock in the morning, dismissed for lunch at 12, and reassembled at 2 and continued to 4 o'clock. They were largely attended by the faithful of each church, and by the curious of no church, and invariably left the community as much divided on the question of creed as before."

Izard County has been a leader in the production of preachers. Some of the best preachers in this and many other states were born and reared in Izard County. Leaders in the Baptist faith include A. B. Cooper, Stanley Cooper, Hugh Cooper, Roscoe Cooper, Melvin Wiles, Sidney Wiles, Amos Muncy, Luther Muncy (D.D. degree, college professor, author of several books, and now a missionary to South America), Ezekiel Sherrill (widely known evangelist and debater), Ed Sherrill, W. M. Cooper, H. F. Vermillion (not a native of the county but spent much of his life here), J. M. Rush and W. H. McCuistion. Church of Christ: Joe Warlick (nationally known debater, writer and evangelist), Will Schultz (foreign missionary and said to have memorized the Bible), T. H. Sherrill, Frank Puckett, Harrison Porterfield and Oscar Billingsley. Among the Presbyterians must be mentioned Elbert Conyers, who was for a time missionary to South America. Among the outstanding Methodist preachers the county has given to other states are Burl Long and Hayden Sears. Some of the older residents of the county remember such early patriarchs as "Uncle Henry" Hays, M. B. Umstead, Jim Bone, Bob Evans, "Uncle Billy" Duren, R. T. Farthing and many others whose names are dimmed by time, but whose works will live forever.

PRESENT COUNTY OFFICIALS

J. A. RODMAN, county judge, was born near Newburg August 13, 1908. He was elected sheriff and collector in 1940, and re-elected in 1942. During his second term as sheriff, he entered the army May 2, 1944, and was discharged October 19, 1945. He was elected judge in 1946, and entered upon his duties January 1, 1947. He was county roll call chairman of the American Red Cross from 1941 to '43.

Mr. Rodman quit school after completing the eighth grade and began hustling for himself. He farmed, dealt in livestock and operated a cotton gin for years. At present he is a partner with A. J. Younger in the Younger Motor Company, Melbourne; a partner with E. D. Peacock in Peacock Drug Company, also in Melbourne, and owns stock in the Bandmill Gin Company. He also owns about 2,000 acres of land in Izard County.

H. D. Stuart, clerk and recorder, was born near Wiseman February 24, 1907. He started his political career in the office of tax assessor to which he was elected in 1938. He served three terms, but during the last term he was inducted into the army May 1, 1944, and served until September 11, 1945. He was elected to his present position in 1946, taking office January 1, 1947.

Previous to his entrance into politics, Mr. Stuart taught school in the county about 10 years. During this time he completed a year of college above high school, mostly by correspondence courses.

Before entering the army, he received a citation award for his activities connected with the Red Cross and War Bond sales.

Boyce J. Cook, sheriff and collector, was born at Melbourne December 25, 1919, son of Mr. and Mrs. J. H. Cook. After completing Melbourne High School in 1938, he worked with the N. Y. A. about four years. He entered the army January 22, 1942, and was advanced to staff sergeant before he was discharged September 25, 1945. He was in six major campaigns—African, Sicilian, Naples-Foggia, Rome-Anzio, Southern France and the Rhineland—and was overseas nearly three years. He was awarded six bronze stars and the good conduct medal.

Mr. Cook was elected sheriff and collector in 1946, which was his first time to ask for a public office. He began his duties January 1, 1947.

Dale Estes, tax assesor, was born at Melbourne December 26, 1906, a son of the late R. J. Estes and Mrs. Lena Estes. He didn't exactly cut his baby teeth on a type-stick, but began work in his father's printing office (*The Melbourne Times*) at the age of eight. He worked in the *Times* office 20 years, under three ownerships—R. J. Estes, E. A. Smith and Karr Shannon. After this, he worked as clerk of the W. P. A. for three years. In 1940 he was elected county treasurer, serving two terms. He was elected tax assessor in 1944, and was re-elected in 1946, now serving his second term.

J. D. Marchant, treasurer, was born at Lunenburg January 29, 1913, son of the late Mr. and Mrs. Oscar Marchant. He attended the Lunenburg grade school and the Melbourne

High School. He was inducted into the army October 12, 1944, and received his discharge April 10, 1946. He was elected treasurer in 1946 and began his duties January 1, 1947. This is his first time to serve in public office.

George W. Howard, coroner, was born July 26, 1885, in Marion County. He moved to Melbourne from Alicia, Lawrence County, in November, 1926. He was mayor of Melbourne, 1937-39. He was elected coroner the first time in August, 1944, and re-elected in 1946. He is a minister of the church of Christ and has served a number of churches in and out of the county.

Remmel Billingsley, surveyor, was born at Franklin January 1, 1913. He attended the Franklin and Melbourne high schools, graduating from the latter in 1930. He has completed about three years of college, much of which was by correspondence from the University of Arkansas. He has taught in the grade schools of Myron, Jumbo and Hickory Flat, and in the Melbourne and Mt. Pleasant high schools, and at this writing is under contract to teach at Mammoth Spring, Fulton County. He began serving as county surveyor in 1945.

Gus H. Campbell, county welfare director, was born at Melbourne April 8, 1910, son of Mr. and Mrs. J. D. Campbell. He graduated from Melbourne High School in 1929, and was graduated from Arkansas Polytechnic College, Russellville, in 1931. He attended the University of Arkansas from 1933 to 1935, completing a major in social science. He taught social science and Latin in Melbourne High School for two years. He was employed by the W. P. A. and the Resettlement Administration from 1937 to 1939. He became county welfare director in 1939, serving until April 7, 1942, when he entered the army. He was discharged December 27,

1942, with the rank of corporal. He was employed by the State Labor Department, Division of Employment Security, from January 2 to May 17, in 1943, and since that time has been the county welfare director.

Tom Simpson, county school supervisor, was born at Franklin January 1, 1907, the son of the late T. W. Simpson and Mrs. Sallie Simpson. After completing school at Franklin, he attended the University of Arkansas and State College at Jonesboro. He was formerly superintendent of the Violet Hill High School and the Melbourne High School. He became county examiner in 1937 and has served continuously as head of the county's schools since then, except for a few months served in the army during World War II.

Mr. Simpson has also had business connections the past several years, being for some years a partner with H. E. Bursey in the Oklahoma Tire & Supply Company at Melbourne, and also has stock in the cold storage plant recently constructed at Melbourne. He is an outstanding civic leader, and usually plays an important part in any public move for the benefit of his community or county.

John R. Hamilton, representative, was born near Oxford March 3, 1889. He finished the grade schools at that place and attended Sloan-Hendrix Academy, Imboden, two years. For several years he helped manage the farm and livestock interests of C. C. Aylor. He began selling automobiles in 1927. During the past 20 years he has worked for several firms and is an outstanding salesman. At present he is operating his own used car agency.

Mr. Hamilton was elected the county's representative in 1946 and served in the 1947 session of the state Legislature. This is his first venture in the field of politics. He was ordained a Baptist preacher in 1945.

TENURE OF COUNTY OFFICERS

THE FOLLOWING is a list of the names of the county officers of Izard County, and the dates of their terms of service from the organization of the county to the present time:

Judge—Matthew Adams, 1829-33; J. Jeffery, 1833-38; B. Hawkins, 1840-42; J. A. Harris, 1842-44; James Wren, 1844-46; J. A. Harris, 1846-48: G. H. Morton, 1848-50; Henry Cole, 1850-52; J. J. Same, 1852-54; B. F. Hollowell, 1854-56; T. Black, 1858-60; H. H. Harris, 1860-62; Thomas Black, 1862-64; A. C. Jeffery, 1864-68; William Byler, 1868-74; G. W. Shaw, 1874-80; J. A. Ryler, 1880-82; W. Grimmett, 1882-86; H. H. Harris, 1886-92; G. S. Rector, 1892-96; C. C. Haley, 1896-1900; T. J. Ashley, 1900-04; M. H. Hays, 1904-08; William Halbrook, 1908-10; P. C. Sherrill, 1910-14; W. D. Wallace, 1914-19; C. C. Aylor, 1919-23; W. W. Copeland, 1923-27; C. C. Aylor, 1927-33; J. D. Hames, 1933-35; John W. Hammett, 1935-39; C. C. Aylor, 1939-41; W. E. Billingsley, 1941-47; J. A. Rodman, 1947-.

Clerk—J. P. Houston, 1825-30; Jesse Adams, 1830-32; J. P. Houston, 1832-38; B. H. Johnston, 1838-44; C. P. Lancaster, 1844-46; A. C. Jeffery, 1846-48; R. M. Haggard, 1848-52; William Wood, 1852-54; H. H. Harris, 1854-58; W. C. Dixon, 1858-66; H. H. Harris, 1866-68; I. H. Talley, 1868-72; F. W. Perrin, 1872-74; D. W. Billingsley, 1874-76; J. N. Craig, 1876-78; H. H. Harris, 1878-84; W. K. Estes, 1884-90; A. C. Dixon, 1890-94; W. K. Estes, 1894-1900; E. A. Billings-

HISTORY OF IZARD COUNTY

ley, 1900-02; Ed. Billingsley, 1902-04; W. K. Estes, 1904-06; T. F. Allen, 1906-10; A. P. Golden, 1910-14; T. H. Linn, 1914-19; C. C. Haley, 1919-23; V. C. Holloway, 1923-25; J. W. Hall, 1925-29; J. D. Hames, 1929-33; W. E. Billingsley, 1933-37; E. J. Williams, 1937-41; R. G. Miller, 1941-45; E. J. Williams, 1945-47; H. D. Stuart, 1947-.

R. G. Miller entered the armed services and his wife became acting clerk April 1, 1944, serving the remainder of the term.

Sheriff and Collector—John Adams, 1825-30; John Hargrove, 1830-35; Daniel Jeffery, 1835-36; J. A. Harris, 1836-38; D. K. Loyd, 1838-44; Miles Jeffery, 1844-46; S. E. Rossen, 1846-50; S. J. Mason, 1850-56; John Woods, 1856-58; A. Adams, 1858-60; W. J. Cagle, 1860-68; R. L. Landers, 1868-72; J. M. Hinkle, 1872-78; R. L. Landers, 1878-82; J. S. Roberts, 1882-86; R. L. Landers, 1886-90; T. J. Williamson, 1890-94; D. S. Freeman, 1894-96; T. J. Williamson, 1896-98; D. S. Freeman, 1898-1900; J. A. Harris, 1900-04; P. A. Billingsley, 1904-08; W. A. Wilson, 1908-12; P. A. Billingsley, 1912-16; W. T. Clem, 1916-20; G. R. Landers, 1921-25; R. J. Estes, 1925-27; D. O. Johnson, 1927-31; R. J. Estes, 1931-33; J. A. Harris, 1933-37; W. E. Billingsley, 1937-39; D. O. Johnson, 1939-41; J. A. Rodman, 1941-45; Lawrence Harber, 1945-47; Boyce Cook, 1947-.

R. J. Estes died in August, 1932, and G. R. Landers was appointed August 10 of the same year as acting sheriff, and completed the term.

D. O. Johnson died in July, 1940. His son, Van P. Johnson, was appointed acting sheriff August 1, 1940, and served the remainder of the term.

J. A. Rodman entered the armed services May 2, 1944. Lawrence Harber was appointed to serve the remainder of the term. Rodman had not received his discharge at the time of the next election. Harber was elected without an opponent.

On December 5, 1945, Sheriff Harber was killed by Rubert Byler while Harber was in line of duty as an officer. His wife was appointed acting sheriff to complete the term.

Treasurer—W. B. Carr, 1836-38; A. Creswell, 1838-40; S. H. Creswell, 1840-42; Jacob Wolf, 1842-44; A. McFelich, 1844-46; H. J. Wren, 1846-48; H. Dillard, 1848-50; William Gray, 1850-58; J. W. Cypert, 1858-64; H. H. Harris, 1864-66; E. D. Hays, 1866-68; B. F. Brantley, 1868-72; J. B. Hunt, 1872-74; L. C. Holmes, 1874-76; A. J. Hutson, 1876-80; John McElmurry, 1880-82; H. H. Hinkle, 1882-84; John McElmurry, 1884-86; J. B. Hunt, 1886-94; J. H. Greer, 1894-96; Jeffery Dixon, 1896-98; B. F. Davis, 1898-1902; George T. Cone, 1902-06; Walter McCollum, 1906-10; W. Carter, 1910-12; J. H. Garner, 1912-16; B. F. Shirley, 1916-20; R. J. Estes, 1921-25; A. P. Finley, 1925-29; R. E. Evans, 1929-33; E. J. Williams, 1933-37; R. G. Miller, 1937-41; Dale Estes, 1941-45; Henry Muncy, 1945-47; J. D. Marchant, 1947-.

Coroner—H. C. Roberts, 1829-30; J. Blythe, 1830-35; Jesse Adams, 1835-36; H. W. Bandy, 1840-42; R. C. Moore, 1842-48; G. W. Neal, 1848-50; J. D. Churchill, 1850-52; D. Jeffery, 1852-54; R. Harris, 1854-56; S. T. Martin, 1856-58; R. Landers, 1858-62; Jesse Hinkle, 1862-64; J. A. Byler, 1864-66; R. Landers, 1866-68; J. G. Richardson, 1868-72; J. H. Roten, 1872-74; J. F. Cornelius, 1874-76; F. M. Hall, 1876-78; Squire Wood, 1878-80; J. R. Beaver, 1880-86; John Schell, 1886-88: S. F. Reaves, 1888-90; John Schell, 1890-92; R. J. Wheeler, 1892-94; H. H. Harris, 1896-1902; J. H. Newsom, 1902-04; Vaught, 1908-10; Dr. H. H. Smith, 1910-16; Dr. W. S. Baldwin, 1916-19; Dr. E. A. Baxter, 1925-27; Dr. H. H. Smith, 1927-29; Dr. R. L. Flemming, 1929-31; Dr. E. A. Baxter,

1931-35; Dr. M. R. Dzierwa, 1935-37; Mason Ellis, 1937-43; C. E. Kabler, 1943-45; G. W. Howard, 1945-.

Surveyor—William Clement, 1830-32; A. Adams, 1835-36; Jesse Adams, 1836-38; James Davis, 1838-40; William Seymour, 1840-42; J. M. Pough, 1842-44; T. M. Copeland, 1844-46; R. Decker, 1846-48; Cyrun Crosby, 1848-52; J. Byler, 1852-56; J. W. Rector, 1856-58; A. C. Hardin, 1858-62; J. W. Rector, 1862-64; J. A. Claiborne, 1864-68; R. Sanders, 1868-72; J. A. Claiborne, 1872-76; Joseph Hixor, 1876-80; Jacob Franks, 1880-82; J. A. Claiborne, 1882-86; E. L. Billingsley, 1888-92; W. H. Pearson, 1892-96; W. B. Harris, 1896-98; E. Benbrook, 1898-1906; Mack Cypert, 1906-08; Jas. Wingate, 1908-10; W. W. Bruce, 1910-14; T. J. Guthrie, 1914-16; G. J. Dillard, 1916-25; Mack Cypert, 1925-31; J. O. Hunt, 1931-32; Loas Jacobs, 1932-33; E. A. Smith, 1933-39; Virgil Coleman, 1939-45; Remmel Billingsley, 1945-.

Mack Cypert died January 19, 1931, and J. O. Hunt was appointed surveyor February 16, 1931. He resigned later and Loas Jacobs was appointed February 27, 1932.

Assessor—P. F. Heasley, 1868-72; W. O. Dillard, 1872-74; James Green, 1874-80; W. H. Hammond, 1880-84; Robert Gray, 1884-86; James Gray, 1886-88; P. J. Puckett, 1888-92; T. A. Pearson, 1892-96; James Gaston, 1896-1900; J. W. Spann, 1900-04; B. F. Shirley, 1904-08; A. H. Benbrook, 1908-12; G. T. Lacy, 1912-14; W. J. Carder, 1914-19; W. A. Jackson, 1919-23; T. W. Puckett, 1923-27; Harry Clark, 1927-31; R. O. Tomlinson, 1931-35; J. O. Hunt, 1935-39; H. D. Stuart, 1939-45; Dale Estes, 1945-.

H. D. Stuart entered the armed services and his wife became acting tax assessor May 1, 1944, to complete the term.

Representative—The first representative of the county in

HISTORY OF IZARD COUNTY

the Territorial Legislature was Jacob Wolf. Representatives in the state legislatures served the following years: Thomas Culp, 1836-38; (none), 1838-40; W. M. Wolf, 1840-42; Jehoida Jeffery,· 1842-44; Thomas Riggs, 1844-46; Daniel Jeffery, 1846-48; Thomas Riggs, 1848-50; S. E. Rosson, 1850-52; Thomas Black, 1852-54; John A. Beck, 1854-56; Miles Jeffery, 1856-60; Thomas W. Edmonston, 1860-62; R. H. Powell, 1862-64; J. B. Brown, 1864-66; W. C. Dixon, 1866-68; (none), 1868-70; F. J. Eubanks, 1870-72; Joseph Wright, 1872-74; E. O. Wolf, 1874-76; John W. C. Gardner, 1876-78; W. E. Davidson, 1878-80; Thomas Black, 1880-82; W. E. Davidson, 1882-84; J. B. Baker, 1884-86; George Ferguson, 1886-88; D. D. Shaver, 1888-90; J. B. Baker, 1890-92; Ransom Gulley, 1892-94; Wiley Croom, 1894-96; William B. Hamm, 1896-98; Granville S. Rector, 1898-1902; A. C. Dixon, 1902-04; Thomas J. Ashley, 1904-06; J. D. Lackey, 1906-08; R. D. Harris, 1908-10; J. D. Lackey, 1910-12; W. W. Copeland, 1912-21; Ben Hassell, 1921-23; J. P. Cook, 1923-27; T. R. Wilson, 1927-29; Tillman E. Lawrence, 1929-33; W. W. Copeland, 1933-37; R. H. Wood, 1937-39; W. E. Billingsley, 1939-41; Guy Gaston, 1941-43; R. L. Blair, 1943-47; John Hamilton, 1947-.

According to the records in the office of Secretary of State, Izard County had no representative in the special session of the Confederate Legislature held at Washington, Hempstead County, September 22 to October 2, 1864.

State Senate—According to the best records available, the following Izard County men have served in the state Senate: C. R. Sanders, 1836-40; S. E. Rosson, 1856-62; H. C. Tipton, 1876-86 (Tipton is also said to have lived in Baxter and may have been elected from that county); W. E. Davidson, 1892-96; Granville S. Rector, 1904-08; John C. Ashley, 1913-17; E. E. Godwin, 1917-21; John C. Ashley, 1933-37; J. Orville Cheney, 1945-.

HISTORY OF IZARD COUNTY

From the time Izard County was created, the senatorial district in which it was situated changed nine times. From 1836 to 1840, the district was made up of Carroll, Searcy and Izard counties. From 1840 to 1844, it was Izard and Lawrence. In 1844 to 1848, it was Izard, Van Buren and Fulton. In 1848 to 1856, it was Independence and Izard. Then Van Buren and Izard made up the district from 1856 to 1866. On that year it became known as the "Ninth District," and these two counties made up the district for two years more. The "Third District" was formulated in 1868, consisting of Madison, Marion, Carroll, Fulton and Izard counties. This district continued until 1874 when it was changed to the "Twenty-third District," with a combination of Fulton, Izard, Marion and Baxter counties. In 1905 Marion County was cut out, leaving Fulton, Izard and Baxter. This combination continued until 1938 when it was changed to the "Eleventh District" with Fulton, Izard, Stone, Van Buren and Cleburne counties.

MODERN IZARD COUNTY

TODAY, IZARD COUNTY is one of the progressive areas of the South. It has good schools and churches, active civic organizations, fine homes and farms, and a spirit of neighborliness that reaches into every nook and corner. Mercantile establishments, banks, garages, theaters and other business enterprises keep pace with the forward trend of the better communities of the nation.

A network of highways and all-weather roads throughout the county offer immeasurable conveniences to the farmer. He can sell his livestock, milk, cream, chickens and eggs to local buyers or truck them to near-by markets. Hogs and cattle are the leading commercial species of livestock raised. In recent years the dairy industry has reached unprecedented proportions. There are a number of milk routes in the county, and farmers sell thousands of dollars worth of milk monthly.

Most of the soil is limestone underlaid with red clay. Some of the land in the county has been in cultivation a hundred years, and is still producing. An extensive soil conservation program during the past several years has put hundreds of farms in first-class shape. Land that has been mistreated can be made productive again with crop rotation and legumes.

Izard County land is very productive and all crops and

fruits raised in the temperate zone can be produced here. Corn, cotton, sorghum and hay crops are leaders. Hogs and cattle can be brought to maturity here as cheaply or more cheaply than in any other section of the United States. Tame grasses will take care of livestock nine to ten months of the year. Pure water for stock is abundant in hundreds of springs and streams.

The climate of the county is invigorating, and health conditions rank above the average for the state. The mean annual temperature is 58.8 degrees and an annual precipitation of about 45 inches makes pasture, fruit, and field crop growing profitable.

With rare exception, all land not in cultivation or pasture is covered with mature timber. The whir of sawmills can be heard from day to day in a number of places. Sawmilling, along with other timber industries, such as bolt and tie and cedar post, furnish regular employment to scores of men.

Electric power is now available to most every town in the county, furnished by the Arkansas Power & Light Company or the R. E. A., and rural electrification is rapidly being extended to every farm home.

Izard County is adjacent to the vast resort area of Lake Norfork, and the county itself is a perfect natural setting for summer vacationists. Here are beautiful streams bordered by pine-scented forests, and low mountains rising majestically from the banks of White River. There are plenty of camping places and good springs. One may cruise along the clear, sparkling waters of White River, and swim and fish. Or he may visit one of the county's caves. The Melbourne Cave down in a wild and rocky ravine of deep forests has a natural arched entrance. Inside is a vast underground world of winding passages that lead into many beautiful chambers with vaulted dome-shaped roofs. Many rooms have wonderful stalactite and stalagmite formations whose natural luster and forms would rival those of any cave in the world. Pilot Knob, one of the highest elevations in the Ozark foothills, is another attraction, from whose summit can be viewed the greater portion of the county's area and miles of territory in some of the border counties.

Izard County is one of the most scenic sections of the state. It ranks among the best in schools, dairying, farm production, and natural resources. Any normal person who is willing to work can make a good living here, and the many school bus routes offer high school opportunities to at least 90 per cent of the children of school age. The county has never had any labor or negro troubles. It is made up chiefly of hard-working, peace-loving, straight-thinking people. No purer strain of Anglo-Saxon blood can be found in any other part of the United States.

MISCELLANEA

THE POPULATION of Izard County is about 13,500; total land area is 373,120 acres; the elevation is about 700 feet.

The county now has only five practicing physicians: Dr. C. L. Harris of Melbourne, Dr. Noel Copp and Dr. Pharr of Calico Rock, Dr. Henry Smith of Oxford, and Dr. Jeff Smith of Violet Hill. There is only one dentist, Dr. H. Meade, of Calico Rock.

There are six attorneys: R. D. Harris and W. E. Billingsley of Melbourne, Guy Wiley of Violet Hill, Claude Caldwell of Oxford, Wiley F. Smith of Calico Rock, and Frank Benbrook of Wideman.

M. H. Hays of Tuckerman was for about five years the only ex-judge of the county until W. E. Billingsley left the office the first of 1947. Yet, he served as the county's judge in 1904 to 1908. He is now about 93 years old.

W. E. Billingsley probably has held the biggest variety of county offices. He was elected clerk in 1932. He was in office continuously until January 1, 1947, holding the offices of clerk, sheriff, representative and judge—and without a single defeat.

The murder of Sheriff Lawrence Harber, December 5, 1945, was the county's top news story since the turn of the century. Sheriff Harber was shot down by Rubert Byler at the Byler home near Jumbo. Byler and his wife hid in the woods for about a month before giving up. Byler was first given the chair, but the Supreme Court reversed the case on technical error, and Byler was finally sentenced to 21 years.

From 1913 to 1917 John C. Ashly served in the state Senate and W. W. Copeland in the lower House. Twenty years later, these same men served in the same capacities for four years.

The White Lime Company of Batesville operated a lime plant a mile below Sylamore for several years. The plant employed dozens of men and some 10,000 barrels of lime were shipped monthly. A town grew up with depot, post office, hotel, store, school and a number of dwellings. Since the lime plant suspended over 15 years ago the town has dwindled away.

Back in the days of the Hoover depression, the American Red Cross handled the relief situation in Izard County just as it did in most other counties throughout the country. The county Red Cross chairman at that time had the biggest job in the county. M. E. Clark, ably assisted by his wife, looked after this for several months. Both worked almost day and night—and gratis. Thousands of dollars worth of food, seed and clothing were dispensed. It was a nerve-wracking task and, in some instances, a thankless one.

Izard County has continuously furnished the judge for the Sixteenth Judicial District since 1914, except for a few months in 1922 when Walter Pope of Pocahontas was appointed to fill out the unexpired term of J. B. Baker, deceased.

Izard County is in Congressional District No. 2, State Senatorial District No. 11, Judicial District No. 16, and Chancery District No. 8.

The present congressman is Wilbur D. Mills of Kensett his wife is a native of Izard County, daughter of Mr. and

Mrs. P. A. Billingsley); the present state senator is J. O. Cheney of Calico Rock; John L. Bledsoe of Pocahontas is circuit judge and Harrell Simpson of Pocahontas is prosecuting attorney; Paul Ward of Batesville is the present chancery judge.

There are about 94 miles of state highways in the county as follows: Highways 9 and 69 (Batesville-Mammoth Spring), passing through Mt. Pleasant, Stella, Sage, Melbourne, Brockwell and Oxford; Highway 56, from Calico Rock to the Sharp County line, passing through Bandmill, Brockwell, Violet Hill, Franklin and Myron; Highway 9, from Melbourne to Sylamore; Highway 58, from near Stella to Sidney, and Highway 5, from Calico Rock to the Baxter County line. There are also about 500 miles of county roads.

The first county farm agent to serve Izard County was W. R. Denton (1912-13). The next was J. F. Drown of Pineville (1914).

The first county welfare director was Miss Eunice Hunt. The next was Mrs. Vada Webb Sheid. Gus H. Campbell is the present director. Other office personnel is composed of Mrs. Mildred Billingsley, home visitor, and Miss Vessie Cooksey, clerk-stenographer. The present County Board of Public Welfare is as follows: I. O. Ford, Homer Harber, W. J. Seay, H. H. Ducker and R. D. Owens. At the time of this writing the department was assisting 502 cases each month with an average monthly pay roll of $8,827.

Following are the county's townships with voting precincts: Athens, Jumbo and Knob Creek; Baker, Wiseman; Barren Fork, Mt. Pleasant; Big Springs, Lower Bone schoolhouse; Bryan, Dolph; Claiborne, Creswell and Gorby; Dry Town, Cedar Grove schoolhouse; Franklin, Franklin; Gid, Gid; Guthrie, Wideman; Guion, Guion; Jefferson, Myron and Day; LaCrosse, LaCrosse and Larkin; Lafferty, Lafferty;

Lunenburg, Lunenburg; Millcreek, Melbourne; Mt. Olive, Mt. Olive; Newburg, Newburg, Brockwell and Bandmill; Newhope, Oxford; Pleasant Hill, Zion and Battles; Sage, Sage; Strawberry, Hickory Flat schoolhouse and Jack schoolhouse; Violet Hill, Violet Hill; White River, Twin Creek and Sylamore; Union, Calico Rock, Pineville and Iuka.

GOVERNOR GEORGE IZARD

A VOLUME on the history of Izard County would not be complete without a sketch of the man for whom the county was named. The following biography was taken from Dallas T. Herndon's *Centennial History of Arkansas*:

"George Izard, the second territorial governor of Arkansas, was born on October 21, 1776, at Richmond, England, where his parents were sojourning. His family were among the early settlers of South Carolina. His father, Ralph Izard, came to America some years before the Revolution. . . . In 1777 he went to Paris and in 1779 returned to America, leaving his family in France, where George received his first schooling. In 1789 the family removed to New York, then the seat of government of the United States, Ralph Izard having been elected one of the first senators from South Carolina. When the meeting of Congress was changed to Philadelphia, George entered the University of Pennsylvania, where he graduated in 1792 at the age of fifteen.

"Shortly after his graduation he was sent to London, in care of Thomas Pinckney, then minister to England, to attend the military schools of Europe. He first entered the Prince of Wales' Royal Military Academy at Kensington, but remained there only a short time. In September, 1792, he became a student in a military school at Marburg, Germany. His next school was the Ecole du Genie, an institution for teaching the art of military engineering, located at Metz. While here he received a commission as lieutenant in the

United States artillery and engineers, and in 1797 returned to America. The Secretary of War placed him in charge of the construction of Castle Pinckney, in Charleston Harbor, as engineer. In 1799 he was promoted to captain and in 1802 was placed in command of the post at West Point. In April, 1803, he resigned his commission and retired to private life.

"Early in 1812, when war with England became imminent, George Izard was commissioned colonel and placed in command of the Second Regiment of Artillery. The following year he was commissioned brigadier-general and in 1814 was promoted to major-general. Educated in foreign military schools, his 'advanced ideas' did not meet with the approbation of some of the American generals, and toward the close of the year 1814 he retired from the army. He then lived quietly with his family in Philadelphia until appointed governor of Arkansas Territory. The appointment was made March 4, 1825, by President Monroe.

"As governor his life was uneventful. He commenced the organization of the militia, and recommended that an arsenal be located at Little Rock, as trouble seemed imminent with the Indians. The Choctaw and Quapaw and other tribes were removed to reservations while he was in office. . . . He was misunderstood and considered an aristocrat and a martinet, although a few discriminating ones could see his good qualities. . . .

"On March 4, 1828, his three-year term having expired, Governor Izard was reappointed by President Adams, but he did not live to complete his second term. His death occurred on Saturday, November 22, 1828, after an illness of about a month, following an attack of gout. He was buried the following Sunday, with the honors of war, in the old cemetery, where the Peabody Public School was afterward built. When Mount Holly cemetery was established in 1843, his remains were removed there and interred in the Ashley burial enclosure. An unpretentious marble slab, the inscription dimmed by time, marks his last resting place."

Thus the man for whom Izard County was named was one of the best educated men ever to serve the state as governor. He studied in some of the best educational institutions here and abroad. He was an excellent governor, and is known for organizing the territory, which previously had merely been drifting along.

It was Governor Izard who settled the spelling of the word "Arkansas." The name had been spelled in various ways. He proved that the name of the territory came from the name of the Arkansa Indians and should be spelled with an "s" at the end instead of a "w."

His hobby was collecting razors. He had collected many different kinds of razors, and shaved with a different one each day of the week.

A portrait of Governor Izard was presented to Izard County by the General George Izard Chapter, Daughters of 1812, of Little Rock, in 1947. The portrait is a copy of an original which was painted in 1813.

Part II

Biographies

HISTORY OF IZARD COUNTY

JOHN C. ASHLEY was born December 31, 1884, at Elizabeth, Fulton County, but at an early age moved with his parents to a farm near Violet Hill. Here he worked on his father's farm and attended rural schools. After attending Melbourne High School in 1905-06, he entered the preparatory department of the University of Arkansas and received his A. B. degree from that institution in 1911. He was one of the top-ranking students in his class. During the time he was not attending school he taught in the rural schools of Sharp, Independence and Izard counties from 1903 to 1911. He was principal of the Evening Shade High School in 1911-12. He then served as superintendent of the Melbourne High School two terms. He quit teaching to attend the Cumberland University Law School at Lebanon, Tennessee. After being admitted to the bar, he opened office at Melbourne and practiced here the remainder of his life.

Mr. Ashley was elected state senator of the 23rd Senatorial District in 1913, serving until 1917. He was then elected prosecuting attorney of the Sixteenth Judicial District and served three terms. He was elected circuit judge of this district in 1922, serving two terms. He made an unsuccessful race for Congress in the Second District in 1930, and entered the governor's race in 1936 but withdrew before the election. He also served another term in the state senate, from 1932 to 1936, and served as a member of the state Forestry Commission under the administration of Governor Carl E. Bailey.

He was president of the Bank of Melbourne at the time of his death, in June, 1943, with which institution he had been officially connected since 1923. He had extensive farming and livestock interests in the county. He served for many years as a member of the local school board, and until his health failed was active in civic, church and community affairs of the county. His widow makes her home at Melbourne. His son, John Ashley, Jr., a major in World War II, is in business here.

C. C. AYLOR, who served the county 12 years as judge, was born at Larkin February 28, 1885. He early followed the vocation of farming, dividing his time between this work and attending the common schools of the county. He taught in the rural schools of the county for 10 years. He first became county judge in 1919, serving two terms. In 1926 he was elected again and served three terms. He was elected once more in 1938 and served one term.

He had official connection with the Bank of Melbourne for several years, and was president of the institution at the time of his death November 14, 1941. He also had extensive land possessions. His widow still makes her home at Melbourne.

JAMES B. BAKER was born June 30, 1856, in Missouri. At the age of nine he moved with his father, Wilson Baker, to Izard County and located near Franklin. After attending the elementary schools of Izard County for three years, young Baker attended the LaCrosse Collegiate Institute. He then engaged in teaching for seven years. In 1884 he began the study of law. His chief coaching was done by Melbourne lawyers. He also took a correspondence course in law from a school in Nashville and received his diploma. He was admitted to the bar at Melbourne in 1889 before Judge Powell. He was later admitted to the United States Court.

Mr. Baker's connection with active politics began with his appointment as clerk of the lower house of the Arkansas Legislature in 1883. In 1884 he was elected to the Legislature and was elected again in 1890. In 1892 he was elected prosecuting attorney for the judicial district including Izard County, and succeeded himself in this capacity in 1894, serving two terms. When this official career ended he continued the practice of law and engaged in other political activities. He was presidential elector in 1896. He made the race for attorney general of Arkansas in 1898 and was defeated by Jeff Davis in the convention by only one vote. He was a delegate to the National Democratic Convention in 1904 when Alton B. Parker was made the standard bearer of the party for president. He was a familiar figure in all state conventions for thirty years.

Mr. Baker was elected mayor of his home town, Melbourne, three times and was on the school board in this district for more than fifteen years. He was connected with the organization of the Bank of Melbourne and was elected the first cashier after the stock was taken over by Izard County people in 1897. He was elected president of the bank in 1905, in which capacity he served until his death. He was one of the founders of the Union Bank and Trust Company of Batesville, in which institution he was a stockholder and director. He was one of the promoters of the Mississippi Valley Life Insurance Company of Little Rock, and he also stood in such capacity to the Home Life and Guaranty Company of Fordyce. He was a stockholder in the Red Bud Realty Company of Cotter and also helped to finance and bring into existence other concerns.

In fraternal affairs Mr. Baker enjoyed a distinction held by no other citizen of the state at the time, having held the chief state office in the bestowal of two important lodges. He was a Mason and an Odd Fellow. Beginning in the Masonic Grand Lodge in 1880, he was advanced from year to year, until in 1897 he was elected Grand Master of Arkansas. In the same year he was also elected Grand Master of Odd Fellows from the floor of the Grand Lodge.

On October 31, 1914, Mr. Baker took up the duties of circuit judge of the Sixteenth Judicial Circuit. He remained in this capacity until his death in 1922.

DR. F. A. BAXTER was born in Batesville in 1853, a son

of Elisha D. Baxter, later governor of Arkansas. Hence he came of a family already famed in the early history of the state. But Dr. Baxter's greatness did not lean on that of his ancestors. He attained his own distinction in his practice of medicine.

Dr. Baxter attended the schools of Batesville and there received a good common school education. In 1877 he entered the University of Louisville, from which he graduated in March, 1879. He then returned to his home at Batesville, but remained only a short time, coming to Melbourne the same year. Here he began the practice of his profession and was a faithful servant of humanity until his death.

Dr. Baxter served as health officer of Izard County for several years, and was also coroner for two years. He had a pleasant social disposition that won for him many friends. Kind and obliging, open-hearted and free-handed, he was ever found at the bedside of the sick and helpless. He took no active part in politics and voted always as a matter of duty for what he thought the best interest of his county. He was a Republican, though he voted with the Democratic party often in state and county elections.

Dr. Baxter kept abreast the latest developments in medical science by constant study, and was highly respected in the profession. He died September 12, 1941.

JOHN L. BLEDSOE was born at Old Philadelphia (now Larkin) January 11, 1888. After attending school at Philadelphia and Melbourne, he entered the University of Arkansas from which he graduated in 1910. He was admitted to the practice of law August 25, 1913. He taught school for three years. He was elected to the Constitutional Convention of 1918 from Izard County. He began the practice of law in Melbourne, and for a time was in partnership with the late Judge John C. Ashley. Later he continued the practice of law at Calico Rock. He and his family moved to Pocahontas, Randolph County, in January, 1923. He has been judge of the 16th Judicial District since January 1, 1931.

S. MARCUS BONE, circuit judge of the Third Judicial District, was born near Barren Fork (now Mt. Pleasant) June 29, 1887. After attending the grade school in his home district, he finished high school at Cave City in 1907. He taught school a couple of years and then entered Valparaiso University, Valparaiso, Indiana, from which he graduated in 1911 with the LL.B. degree. He then moved to Batesville where he still makes his home. He began the practice of law January 1, 1912. He served as state senator from his home district from 1919 to 1924. He was elected circuit judge in 1926, and is now serving his sixth four-year term on the bench. He was presidential elector from the Second Congressional District in 1924. He served 10 years on the State Board of Education, from 1931 to '41.

P. A. BILLINGSLEY was born May 22, 1874, near Violet Hill. He attended the home district school, the North Arkansas Academy at old Philadelphia, and the LaCrosse Collegiate Institute. He began teaching at 17 and taught seven years. He served as Izard County sheriff from 1904 to 1908 and again from 1912 to 1916. He was the youngest sheriff in the state when first elected. He never sought any other political office and was never defeated. He moved to Kensett in 1917 where he was director and traveling salesman for a wholesale grocery for 17 years. He was one time the largest strawberry grower in White County, with 75 acres. He served as chairman of the county board of education of White County for over 10 years. Since 1933, Mr. Billingsley has been field supervisor for the Feed and Seed Loan of the

U. S. Government, and his duties have carried him regularly into Cleburne, Stone, Izard, Fulton, Sharp and Independence counties. He and Mrs. Billingsley now make their home in Batesville.

COMDR. EDWARD BAXTER BILLINGSLEY, son of Mrs. Ed Billingsley and the late Ed Billingsley of Melbourne, was born at Melbourne June 18, 1910. He finished Melbourne High School and two years in the University of Arkansas and then entered the U. S. Naval Academy in 1928 from which he graduated in June, 1932. He was assigned to duty on USS Nevada, duty on China Station October, 1934, to May, 1937, where he served on USS Sacramento; then he went to gunboat, Mindanao, flagship of South China Patrol; then to patrol yacht, Isabel, relief flagship for commander of Asiatic fleet. He had two years duty on heavy cruiser, Chicago, in engineering department followed by two years at U. S. Naval Training Station, Norfolk, Va. In August, 1941, he was assigned to the USS Emmons as engineer officer. The Emmons was commissioned December 5, 1941, at Boston, two days before Pearl Harbor, and engaged in patrol convoy work until the summer of 1942 when operated with the British home fleet at Scapa Flow. In October, 1942, he was made executive officer of the Emmons and took part in the invasion of North Africa. He assumed command of the Emmons July 4, 1943, and assisted in hunting and sinking German submarines in the Mediterranean in May, 1944, for which he was awarded Letter of Commendation by Vice Admiral H. K. Hewitt, commander of Eighth Fleet. He took part in the invasion of Normandy and the bombardment of Cherbough. For these activities he was awarded the Silver Star by Admiral Harold R. Stark, commander of naval forces in Europe. In August, 1944, he participated in invasion of Southern France and was awarded the Bronze Star by Vice Admiral Hewitt. He was awarded the Croix de Guerre (with silver star) by the Government of France for the part the Emmons played in the liberation of France. In December, 1944, he was detached from the Emmons and ordered to commissioning and fitting out of USS John H. Bole, a 2,200-ton destroyer. The Bole was commissioned March 3, 1945, and arrived at Okinawa the following June 29, where it served on picket duty until the Japanese surrender. He continued as commander of the Bole until September 16, 1946. He then took a post-graduate course in Personal Administration and Training at Northwestern University from which he graduated with the M. A. degree in June, 1947.

KIRBY BILLINGSLEY, member of the *Wenatchee Daily World* staff for 25 years, was born near Franklin October 11, 1903, son of Mr. and Mrs. David L. Billingsley and grandson of former Congressman Sam B. Hill. He moved West with his parents at an early age and went to work for the *Wenatchee Daily World,* Wenatchee, Washington, in 1918. He served as city editor of the paper for several years.

About two years ago he got a leave of absence from the paper and accepted a position with the Washington state government as assistant director of the Department of Conservation and Development, and spent some time in Washington, D. C., working on various phases of the Columbia River development program. He is a director of the Greater Wenatchee Irrigation District, a Chelan County public utility district commissioner, member of the governor's advisory commission and chairman of the subcommittees of the Alaskan highway and aviation, executive committeeman of the Public Ownership League of Washington, a member of the North Central Washington Museum Board and of the Wenatchee Chamber of Commerce, and president of the Columbia River Development League.

During the past several years Mr. Billingsley has been

instrumental in the development of many projects and enterprises in the state of Washington, and was largely responsible for passage of the bill for an appropriation of $500,000 for an electrometallurgical laboratory for the Northwest.

Mr. and Mrs. Billingsley and their daughter and two sons live at Wenatchee.

DE E. BRADSHAW, past president of the Woodmen of the World, one of the largest insurance societies in America, was born near Sage January 5, 1869. He attended the short terms of school in the old Baptist church on "Nubbin Ridge" and later took courses in the LaCrosse Collegiate Institute. From 17 to 21 he taught school at Sage, Lunenburg and Newburg. Later he sold books in Monroe County and also tried his sales ability on a patented ditching machine. He had a hard row to hoe and took most any kind of job at which he could earn a few honest dollars. With his savings he entered the National Normal University of Lebanon, Ohio, and graduated with the B. S. degree in 1891.

After graduation he went to Detroit and traveled in Michigan for a publishing company for a year and a half. He moved to Little Rock and began clerking in the law office of Col. Sam W. Williams in 1892. He joined a group of young men under Prof. Gore in the organization of the law school of the University of Arkansas, conducted then and for some time as a night school. He graduated in 1894 with the LL.B. degree. He then entered actively into the practice of law with Sam W. Williams. The records of the Supreme Court of Arkansas show that for the following 22 years, he was an advocate in many important lawsuits which reached the high court. He practiced law alone for several years and then formed the partnership of Bradshaw, Rhoton & Helm.

Mr. Bradshaw assisted in the organization of the Peoples

Savings Bank, the City Realty Company, and many other Little Rock corporations. He served on the Pulaski County Democratic Central Committee and was one of the election commissioners of that county for many years, but was never a candidate for public office. He sponsored and organized the Arkansas Bar Association in 1898 which has continuously functioned since that time. He was active in church affairs, and served as chairman of the Arkansas Sunday School Association, and as president of the Arkansas Humane Society.

Mr. Bradshaw became active in the local camp of the Woodmen of the World in Little Rock and was elected Head Consul in 1899 for the states of Arkansas, Louisiana and Mississippi. In March of the same year he was elected to the national office as director. He served continuously as a member of the board of directors of the W. O. W. until 1916.

In October, 1916, he accepted the position of general attorney for the W. O. W. which necessitated his moving from Little Rock to Omaha, Nebraska. During the 16-year period of service as general attorney he tried many of the most important cases which have arisen in this country involving the authority of fraternal societies.

On November 30, 1932, he was unanimously elected president of the W. O. W. After serving for more than 11 years in which the company made great strides in improvement, he resigned to become chairman of the board of directors of the W. O. W. which position he still holds.

To enumerate the many other things Mr. Bradshaw did as a civic leader and builder in Nebraska would be to write a volume. The family still lives at Omaha.

ROBERT BURNS, the only Izard County native to serve as governor of a state, was born near Oxford August 13, 1874. The biography of this man reads like the story of Abraham

Lincoln. Mr. Burns was born in a log cabin which had a dirt floor. Because of poor finances he was not able to enter school until he was 17. He learned to read from almanacs and borrowed books. The family was not able to buy kerosene, so young Burns would read by the light from the pine-knots burning in the big fireplace.

At the age of 21 he passed the teachers' examination, and thereafter taught in several of the county's one-room schools. In spare time he studied law and did manual labor between school terms. For a time he served as deputy clerk under W. K. Estes. He and Wm. A. Oldfield were admitted to the bar at the same time, in 1899. He then attended the Nashville College of Law from which he graduated with the LL.B. degree.

In 1902 three doctors told Mr. Burns he had tuberculosis, and he headed West, stopping in the Oklahoma territory for a few months and then on to Gold Beach, Oregon. He was admitted to the Oregon Supreme Court bar in March, 1903. Between odd jobs he began picking up a law practice. He was elected to the Oregon Legislature in 1904, the first Democrat elected from Coos and Curry counties in 25 years. He taught school at Gold Beach in the winter of 1903-04. He moved back to Oklahoma territory in 1905 and had an important part in shaping the Constitution for the coming state of Oklahoma. He was elected prosecuting attorney in the new state in 1906 and served until 1911. He did not seek re-election.

He bought a law office in Oklahoma City and moved there in 1913. He was elected state senator in 1916. In 1918 he was elected prosecuting attorney of Oklahoma County. He did not seek re-election. In 1926 he opened a law office in Seminole, a new booming oil town, and a year later was appointed municipal counselor by the governor, which position he held four years. He was elected lieutenant

HISTORY OF IZARD COUNTY

governor in 1930 for a four-year term, during which time he served four and one-half months as acting governor. In 1940 he was elected to the state senate. He was re-elected in 1944. In September, 1946, he moved back to Oregon and formed a law partnership with Albert A. Asbahr at Portland.

Mr. Burns and his wife (formerly Miss Effie Harber, also an Izardite) have seven children living and four dead. Three of the four sons saw action in World War II. The other was with the F. B. I. for three and one-half years.

When in the Oklahoma state senate in 1917 Mr. Burns was instrumental in the establishment of the State University Hospital in Oklahoma City, the nucleus around which the medical school has been built. In recognition of this service, the faculty and student body of the medical school on March 27, 1947, tendered a banquet in his honor. In November, 1946, he was elected a member of the Oklahoma Historical Society Hall of Fame for distinguished public service to the state. Only four were elected, three of whom were Arkansans.

R. L. BLAIR has probably had one of the busiest careers of any Izardite on record. He has served 12 years as cashier of the Bank of Melbourne, four years as mayor of the town, six years as city recorder, eight years on the town council, 15 years on the local school board, four years as secretary of the Chamber of Commerce, was treasurer of the Izard County Chapter of the American Red Cross, and chairman of the county U. S. O. and county War Bond chairman throughout World War II, served one term on the State Board of the Arkansas Farm Bureau Federation, two years as president of the Izard County Farm Bureau, and two terms in the Arkansas Legislature (1943-47). He is now serving on the county Board of Education, and is manager of Landers & Company, owning half-interest in the business. In addition to this, he looks after several farms which he owns.

Mr. Blair was born at Lunenburg November 14, 1900. He graduated from Melbourne High School in May, 1920. After this, he completed a course in Springfield Business College, and began his business career as bookkeeper in the store he now manages.

THE BABER FAMILY. Probably there are few families in Arkansas that can boast of five members as graduates of the University of Arkansas—all from the same department. But that is the case of the Dr. C. T. Baber family which grew up in a remote section of Izard County, near Myron.

There were eight children in the family—five boys and three girls. They all attended the university, with the five boys graduating from the College of Agriculture.

Q. M. and L. C. Baber finished the same year—1925. L. C. is now managing director of the South Central Chain Stores' Council, with headquarters in Little Rock, a position he has held for six years. For 15 years prior to that time he was associated with the University Extension Service.

Q. M. Baber is now a teacher in vocational agriculture at Malvern, where he has been since 1931. Prior to that time he taught at Lamar, in Johnson County, and Morrilton, Conway County.

J. C. Baber was graduated in 1928 and taught vocational agriculture at Huntsville from 1928 to 1944. Since that time he has been teaching agriculture at Siloam Springs.

E. O. Baber completed his work in the university in 1936, and for the last eight years has been associated with the Chilean Nitrate Sales Corporation in charge of its Arkansas territory, except for three years of the time during which he was with the armed services overseas. He formerly was with the Farm Security Administration.

HISTORY OF IZARD COUNTY

H. T. Baber was graduated in 1937. Since that time he has been engaged in vocational agriculture teaching and county extension work. He is serving now as county agent of Union County.

W. W. COPELAND was born June 29, 1873, in the western part of Izard County near Calico Rock. He was reared in the same community, attending the common schools of the county and devoting much of his early life to farming. He completed his education in Melbourne High School, and at the age of 20 began teaching and taught continuously, both winter and summer, for 16 years. He did not teach in a great number of districts of the county, since he taught a number of terms at the same place, and was usually urged to continue teaching in any particular district in which he happened to be employed. He was elected to the Arkansas Legislature in 1912. He ran for a second term without opposition. He was elected to a third term and also to a fourth term. During the time he was in the Legislature he continued the profession of teaching at intervals. He was co-author of the law creating the Batesville-Mammoth Spring highway. In 1922 he was elected county and probate judge, and served two terms.

He was elected to the Legislature again in 1932, serving two more terms. He served in the lower house longer than any other man from Izard County. He died October 27, 1942.

DAVE CRAIGE, one of the pioneer printers of Izard County, was proprietor of the *Izard County Register,* once published at Melbourne, at one time the only paper in the county. Mr. Craige was a native of North Carolina, being born in the year 1836.

At the age of 15 years he commenced serving an apprenticeship at the printer's trade in Lincolnton, North Carolina, and after following this for some time, he came to Batesville, in 1852. Soon after reaching here he went to work on the *Commercial Standard,* a publication run by John C. Claiborne. Mr. Claiborne only ran the paper a year, when he sold it to Urban E. Fort, and the name and political status were changed from Democrat to Whig. The paper then became known as the *Independent Balance,* and was run under that name until the commencement of the Civil War. About 1858 Prof. M. Shelby Kennard assumed control of the publication, and through all the political changes Mr. Craige worked on this paper until the breaking out of the war. On account of poor health he was exempt from service, and during the war and for a few years afterward, he was engaged in farming on North Fork and Piney Bayou. In 1871 he again took up the printing business and worked on the *North Arkansas Times,* a Democrat paper published at Batesville. He continued with this paper until 1873 when he went to Jacksonport and was engaged as a journeyman on the *Statesman,* a Republican journal edited by John Fagan. From 1873 to 1883 Mr. Craige merely rusticated, for his health was quite poor at the time. In 1883 he took charge of the *Sharp County Record* for J. W. Buckley and managed it for three years.

In January, 1887, he came to Izard County and at first leased the *Izard County Register,* but in November, 1888, purchased the paper and ran it in the interest of the Democratic party. He continued the publication until 1907 when he died and the paper seems to have ceased to exist.

J. ORVILLE CHENEY, present state senator from the Eleventh District, was born at Boswell January 30, 1905. After finishing the course of study in the Boswell school, he entered Calico Rock High School from which he graduated. He later attended Arkansas State Teachers College, Conway, and is now taking a correspondence course in law.

He taught in the rural schools of the county for nine years. He was a member of the Izard County board of education from 1942 to 1945. He was a member of the County Advisory Committee of the F. S. A. in 1942, and served on the State Advisory Board in 1943 and '44. He served as district governor of E. A. Y. M. C. in 1945 and '46 and is now county chairman of the American Red Cross. He was elected to the state senate in 1944, and was appointed by Governor Ben Laney as a member of the Board of Trustees of Arkansas State College, Jonesboro, in 1947, to become the first Izardite ever to serve on a state college board.

Mr. Cheney went into the retail drygoods business at Calico Rock in 1933 "on my savings as a country schoolteacher," and now has one of the largest stores in this section of the state.

MACK CYPERT, for many years surveyor of Izard County, was born in the Hidden Creek area, near Lunenburg. After completing the courses in the common schools, he attended the LaCrosse Collegiate Institute for two years. He attended the Southwest Texas State Normal, San Marcos, Texas, in 1915-16. He taught school a total of about 30 years. He first became surveyor of the county in 1906, and served at intervals for years, being in this capacity at the time of his death January 19, 1931.

Mr. Cypert was well read and a pretty good authority on most anything. He was a good stenographer, well versed in both law and engineering, and once wrote a song which sold well as sheet music. He never married.

O. P. ESTES, one-time city judge of Oklahoma City, Oklahoma, was born at Newburg February 2, 1888. He attended district schools at Dillard, Flat Rock and Newburg, and graduated from the Calico Rock High School in 1908. He taught school for five years in Izard, Independence and Jackson counties, farming and sawmilling between terms. In 1910 he completed a business course under J. Denton Guthrie at Calico Rock. He attended the Law Department of Cumberland University, Lebanon, Tennessee, graduating in June, 1916. He passed the bar examinations in both Tennessee and Arkansas the same year.

Mr. Estes moved to Oklahoma City in January, 1917, passed the bar examination in that state, and began working for the law firm of Heiner, Burns and Toney (Robert Burns of Izard County). From 1919 until 1923 he was the junior member of the law firm of Cargill, Looney and Estes. From May, 1923, to May, 1931, he was city judge of Oklahoma City. At present he is devoting his time to the practice of law and looking after real estate and oil holdings he has acquired in Oklahoma and Texas. The family lives in Oklahoma City. Two sons, Bill and Jack, are in military service. The other son, Charles, is attending high school.

R. J. ESTES, famed throughout the world in news dispatches and Ripley's "Believe It or Not" for being elected sheriff of Izard County after his death, was born February 4, 1879, near Melbourne. He began working in the printing office of the old *Izard County Register* at the age of eight. Between terms of school and after school he worked with this paper until a short time after the *Melbourne Times* was established in 1896. He worked for the *Times* several years, and then bought it in 1905. He published the paper 17 years, selling to E. A. Smith in September, 1922.

Mr. Estes was elected county treasurer in 1920 and served two terms, running both the office and newspaper the first two years. He was elected sheriff in 1924, serving one term.

He then worked for the State Highway Department two or three years. In 1930 he was again elected sheriff. He was re-elected August 10, 1932, three days after his death. He was sick throughout the campaign and missed several speaking engagements. When he died the ballots had already been printed and it was too late to recall them. The voters, knowing he was dead, went ahead and nominated him over his opponent, O. L. Elliott. Two different times since then, Ripley portrayed the incident in his "Believe It or Not" cartoon which is published in hundreds of papers throughout the world. Mr. Estes' widow lives at Melbourne.

WILLIAM K. ESTES was born near Melbourne September 5, 1853. He served in the capacity of clerk and recorder of Izard County seven terms, more than any other person in the history of the county. He began serving as deputy clerk in 1876 and continued until 1884 when he was elected clerk. He was re-elected in 1886, and again in 1888. A. C. Dixon then served four years, after which time Mr. Estes was elected again. This time he served three terms, leaving the office in 1900. Four years later he was elected again and served a final term of two years.

After this he never again sought public office. He followed the occupation of farming for a time, including two years in Texas. He returned to Arkansas and went into the mercantile business at Guion. Later he moved to Calico Rock where he began clerking in Garners' Store. He served as postmaster of Calico Rock eight years under the presidential administration of Woodrow Wilson. He then moved back to Melbourne where he served as deputy clerk and notary public for several years. He died in March, 1933. He was a close student of the Bible, and during the last ten years of his life read the New Testament through once each month.

HISTORY OF IZARD COUNTY

JOSEPH T. GARNER, pioneer businessman of Calico Rock, was born in Tennessee March 21, 1865, and moved with the family to Izard County five years later, settling near Oxford. He started his first venture in the mercantile business at Oxford in 1887 with a capital of $85. After a few months he moved his store to Wideman, which was a good trading point at that time. He later re-established his business at Oxford and also put in a business at Hardy.

It was in 1902 that Mr. Garner moved to Calico Rock and started a store. Later, a brother, A. B. Garner, became a partner in the business. The partnership continued until 1926 when they disposed of the business. A few months later of the same year, Mr. Garner opened another store and continued operation until about a year before his death October 12, 1944.

He served as a member of the board of directors of the State Bank of Calico Rock from the time of its organization, and served as vice president of the institution from 1935. He was active in civic and church affairs. His widow still lives at Calico Rock.

RANSOM GULLEY was born in Raleigh, North Carolina, January 24, 1839. He came to Arkansas when a very young man and made his home for many years at Batesville. It was at this place he enlisted in the Confederate army. Mr. Gulley was identified with the life and development of Arkansas for decades and took an active part in many of the history making episodes of Arkansas. He was Izard County's representative to the constitutional convention of 1874. Years later he became engaged in school teaching and followed this profession for some time, teaching for several years in the North Arkansas Academy at Philadelphia. He retired from the teaching profession to take up the practice of law. During this time he also became a successful agriculturalist. He served Izard County in the state Legislature of 1893. Later he was elected State Treasurer and served in this capacity four years, since which time he made his home with his children until his death at the home of his daughter, Mrs. Mary Foster, of Salina, Kansas, in 1921.

J. DENTON GUTHRIE, one of the most able instructors in the county's history, was born near Pineville, but during his childhood his parents moved to Texas where he remained until about the year 1908. He received most of his educational training in the schools and colleges of Texas and upon return to this county he established a business college at Calico Rock. He lost the college and equipment by fire in 1910. He rebuilt on a smaller scale, but later sold the building and continued to carry on his commercial and literary work together at different places where he taught. He headed the Mt. Olive school for eight years and was principal of the Calico Rock High School for the terms of 1923-24 and 1924-25. After this he opened a private school at Calico Rock, which he conducted until September 1926 when he moved to Oxford to continue his work. Although broken in health, and finally having to be assisted to and from school, he carried on virtually to his death January 16, 1927.

As has been said, Mr. Guthrie was a most able instructor and was deeply interested in school work. His prime effort had been in interest of his commercial work, harboring a life ambition for a permanently established commercial school. After completing his commercial studies in Texas he designed a special system of shorthand of his own, which he employed to the exclusion of other systems in fitting score of students for the business world.

F. M. HANLEY, attorney-at-law, was born October 14, 1845, in Graves County, Kentucky.

When 17 years of age he enlisted in the Confederate

army at Camp Boone, near Clarksville, Tennessee, and served in the famous Orphan Brigade until the close of the war and was discharged at Washington, Georgia, May 7, 1865. He participated in all the leading battles in Tennessee and Georgia, including Ft. Donelson, Hartsville, Chickamauga, Jackson, Murfreesboro, Ringold Gap and Missionary Ridge. On September 1, 1864, he was captured by the Federals but was retained only a short time. Previous to this time he was captured at Ft. Donelson, and was held a prisoner from September to February, 1862.

After the close of the war Mr. Hanley returned to Kentucky where he entered school for a short time and then followed the profession of teaching for about three years. He studied law and was admitted to the bar at Mayfield, Kentucky, in 1868, and began the practice of law at that place. In 1873 he came to Phillips County, Arkansas, but on account of poor health, he remained there only a short time, and then came to Izard County, arriving at LaCrosse on the day of the Constitutional election, October 14, 1874. He located there, remaining until the county seat was moved to Melbourne in 1875, when he moved to this place. He resided here and practiced law continuously, except four years during which he served on the Arkansas Railroad Commission, until about 1932 when he retired due to bad health. He died at Batesville at the home of his daughter, Mrs. E. C. Parsons, October 14, 1935.

Mr. Hanley was called "Captain" by his friends, but was not a commissioned officer in the army. The way he happened to be called by the title arose from the fact that after the Orphan Brigade was mounted he was detailed to the commissary department and his comrades dubbed him "Captain" and the title stuck. He was a master at witty sayings and sarcasm—and to this day "Captain" Hanley is often quoted.

HISTORY OF IZARD COUNTY

JAMES A. HARRIS was one of the pioneers of Izard County. He was a native of Georgia and moved to Arkansas in 1820, first locating in Lawrence County, but a short time afterward went to Independence County and there located east of Batesville. After giving his time to farming in that county until 1834, Mr. Harris moved to Izard County, and settled on White River, in Kickapoo Bottom, on the west side of the river in what is now Stone County. Here he purchased 160 acres of land and improved a farm of about 100 acres in the bottom. This bottom was afterwards known as Harris Bottom.

In 1836 he was elected sheriff of Izard County, serving in that capacity for two years, and at a time when it required some little courage to successfully fill the position, as Col. Lewis had recently left with the Cherokee Indians and everything was wild and unsettled. In 1842 he was elected county and probate judge. He was again elected in 1846 and served till his death in 1848. In addition to his political activities he had also followed farming and at the time of his death had acquired considerable property and owned a number of negroes and several hundred acres of well improved farm land.

J. A. HARRIS, a later relative of the former James A. Harris, whose name is mentioned in this volume, was born in Harris Bottom, in what is now Stone County, August 8, 1850. He received a fair education during spare time, but probably never attended school more than six months in all his life, and this six months was spent in the schools of Mt. Olive. At the age of 21 he became constable of White River township, which constituted the beginning of his political activities. He was justice of the peace a total of 42 years and was United States marshal 16 years. He was chief deputy under sheriffs Landers, Hinkle, Roberts, Williamson and Freeman, about 40 years in all. In 1900 he was elected sheriff and was re-elected two years later. He died November 3, 1924.

Mr. Harris was the father of C. L. Harris, practicing physician of Melbourne at present, and James A. ("Jim Butter") Harris, famed as a baseball player in his early days, and serving as sheriff and collector of the county two terms. He has a surviving daughter, Mrs. Clarence Landers, also living at Melbourne.

H. H. HARRIS, son of James A. Harris, was born in Independence County, January 18, 1826. During his boyhood days he assisted on the farm and received his education in subscription schools of the county, later taking a course at Mountain View where he paid fifty cents per week for board. At the age of 18 he began hustling for himself, first doing farm work and horse trading.

In 1854 he was elected county and circuit clerk of Izard County, and re-elected in 1856, serving four years in all. He was then elected county and probate judge, serving until 1862, when he sent in his resignation from Bowling Green, Kentucky, where he had joined the Confederate army, Company G, Eighth Arkansas Infantry. He served east of the Mississippi River and was wounded in the battle of Shiloh, after which he came home and remained about three months. He then went back to the ranks and served until the close of the war. It is said that he was a daring and fearless soldier and participated in some of the closest engagements. He was in the battles of Shiloh, Murfreesboro, Perryville, Chickamauga and Franklin, having been wounded the second time in the last battle. Aside from these he was in many minor engagements. He surrendered at Meridian, Mississippi, in 1865, and returned home.

After his return he again took up farming for some time.

He was then employed to carry the mail and followed this for seven years, after which he entered the mercantile business and was thus occupied from 1871 to 1872, when he moved to LaCrosse and there continued the same business for two years. In 1878 he again became county clerk, was re-elected in 1880 and again in 1882, serving six years in that office. In 1886 he was elected county and probate judge. He was re-èlected twice, serving until 1892. After this time he took no part in politics. He died in 1901.

R. D. Harris, attorney of Melbourne, is a son of H. H. Harris.

SAMUEL BILLINGSLEY HILL, former congressman and now judge of the Tax Court of the United States, was born a mile east of Franklin April 2, 1875. He attended school at Franklin and at the North Arkansas Academy at old Philadelphia, and then entered the University of Arkansas School of Law from which he graduated as an honor student with the LL.B. degree.

He was admitted to the bar in 1898 and began practice at Danville, Yell County, the next year. He was deputy prosecuting attorney for Yell County three years and was mayor of Danville in 1902. He moved to the state of Washington in 1904 and resumed his practice of law. He was elected prosecuting attorney of Douglas County, Washington, in 1906 on the Democratic ticket despite the fact that the county was three-to-one Republican. He was re-elected in 1908. He was elected judge of the Superior Court of the state of Washington in 1916 for a four-year term, and was re-elected without opposition in 1920. He served in this capacity until elected to Congress at a special election in September, 1923, from the Fifth Congressional District of Washington. Although the district was strongly Republican, he continued to be re-elected every two years until he had served in Congress 14 years. He resigned in 1936 to accept an appointment to the United States Board of Tax Appeals which has since been constituted The Tax Court of the United States. He is now serving his 12th year as judge of the court.

While in Congress he served on the Ways and Means Committee, and with such other celebrities as John Nance Garner, Cordell Hull, Henry T. Rainey and Robert L. Doughton. He was an abiding influence on other important committees, and was instrumental in getting through legislation for the construction of the Grand Coulee Dam project which has become nationally known because of the magnitude of its engineering and economic importance.

Mr. Hill served in Congress several years during the tenure of William A. Oldfield, giving Izard County two natives in Congress at the same time, a distinction probably held by no other county in the state.

Mr. Hill is a 32nd degree Mason and a Kappa Sigma. His domicile is Washington state, and his official residence is Washington, D. C.

JEHOIDA JEFFERY came to the White River country from his native Illinois in 1816 and settled two miles above the present site of Mt. Olive. He was a soldier of the War of 1812 and was in the battle of New Orleans under General Jackson. He was also in the service against the Indians between the Missouri River and the upper Mississippi. In a fight with the Indians he encountered a Sioux warrior single-handed and killed and scalped him. He brought this scalp to Izard County.

He was a member of the Territorial Legislature from Independence County about the year 1824, and brought forward the bill creating Izard County. After this he became a member of the Legislature from Izard County and this time brought about a bill to create a new county, Fulton, with territory taken from Izard County. The county was named in honor of the governor at that time.

Mr. Jeffery was judge of Izard County from 1833 to 1838 He died at his home on White River in 1846.

ROBERT EMMETT JEFFERY, the only Izard County native ever to become a minister to a foreign country, was born at Mt. Olive January 30, 1875. After attending schools in the county, he studied law in the office of Ben Williamson, Sr., at Mountain View. He was admitted to the bar in 1899, and moved to Newport and opened a law office in 1903. In 1905 he was elected prosecuting attorney of the Third Judicial District. He served until 1909 when he was elected circuit judge of the district. He was re-elected four years later. Early in 1915 he was named minister to the Republic of Uruguay, South America, by President Woodrow Wilson, and represented the United States in that country until 1921. He died May 19, 1935.

A son, Robert Emmett Jeffery, Jr., is now a lieutenant commander in the U. S. Navy, having graduated from the U. S. Naval Academy at Annapolis, Md., in 1940 and served with distinction in World War II. The other son, Jerry Henry Jeffery, was commander of a B-24 bomber in the Pacific theater during the war. A brother, Forrest Jeffery of Batesville, is now county judge of Independence County. His wife, now Mrs. W. Rexford Brown, still lives at Newport.

D. O. JOHNSON was born in Fulton County March 6, 1886, but moved with his parents to Izard County when very young. He spent his early days attending school and farming in the vicinity of Day. He taught school three years. After serving the county as deputy sheriff about 10 years, he was elected sheriff the first time in 1926, and served two terms. He sought the office again in 1938 and was elected. He died July 28, 1940, several months before his term expired.

Mr. Johnson also served several years as state revenue collector, and was in the automobile business at Melbourne for some time.

WILLIAM RICHARD KENDRICK was born December 8, 1886, on the headwaters of Rocky Bayou, near Melbourne, where he grew to manhood. After finishing school at Melbourne, he completed two years at the University of Arkansas. He graduated in medicine at the Memphis Tennessee University, and practiced some in Izard County in the early 90's. He was a first lieutenant, and later a captain, in the Spanish-American War, 1898. After the war, he returned to Melbourne and clerked in a store for a time.

In 1900 Dr. Kendrick was one of two men in Arkansas to pass an examination as a commissioned officer in the regular peacetime army and, as lieutenant in the infantry, he left Izard County permanently in May, 1900.

He saw service in all possessions of the United States except Alaska, including the Philippine Insurrection, and the Boxer Rebellion in China. In 1910 he was detailed by the President of the United States as professor of Military Science in the University of Georgia, Atlanta. He had been promoted to major in the infantry and, in World War I, was again sent to the Philippine Islands. He became the ranking officer of the islands and for more than a year was acting governor general of the Philippines.

After he returned to the States, he was retired in 1924 with the rank of colonel. After retirement he made his home at Jacksonville, Fla., until his death, which occurred in the Government Faculty at Atlanta, Georgia, January 30, 1941.

OWEN G. KENDRICK, brother of William Richard Kendrick, was born September 22, 1880, at Melbourne. He says he received very little education, getting only to the fifth grade in the Melbourne school. Like his brother, he also served in the Spanish-American War. After the war, he returned to Melbourne and clerked in a store. For a time he was horseback mail carrier on the route from Melbourne to Calico Rock, via Newburg, Benbrook and Pineville; returning via Creswell, Engle and Byler post offices.

For several years he assisted in surveys for railroad routes in several parts of the state, including the White River railroad. In 1904 he became locomotive fireman for the St. Louis Iron Mountain and Southern Railroad. He was transferred to the White River Division in 1906, and has lived at Cotter ever since.

He was promoted from fireman to engineer in 1907. For nearly 40 years, with few misses, he has piloted a locomotive over the White River railroad. He is still in active service on this division of the Missouri Pacific where he is known far and wide as "Happy" Kendrick. He is now operating the Southern Scenic, Kansas City to Memphis fast passenger train, between Cotter and Newport. He is in third place on the Engineers' Seniority Roster.

In 1922, while temporarily out of service with the railroad company, Mr. Kendrick studied law under the late Allyn Smith at Cotter. He was licensed to practice in the state courts in February, 1923. He was later licensed to practice in the Federal courts of the state, and in the U. S. Circuit Court of Appeals, in St. Louis, Missouri.

R. L. LANDERS was born in Tennessee in 1845, and later

moved with his parents to Izard County. He followed the vocation of farming from the time he was old enough to work, attending school between crops. In 1862 he enlisted as a private in Company E, 47th Arkansas Infantry, and served west of the Mississippi River until 1864. He was sergeant of his regiment at the time of his discharge.

In 1868 he was elected sheriff of the county and served two years. In 1878 he was again elected sheriff, and was re-elected in 1880. Two terms were then given to J. S. Roberts, after which Mr. Landers was again elected to the office, and served two more terms. He died in 1913.

He was the father of G. R. ("Roll") Landers who has served the county two terms as sheriff and also served many years as deputy clerk and deputy sheriff.

E. G. LANDERS, one of the pioneer merchants of Izard County, was born in Tennessee May 7, 1846, and came with his parents to Arkansas in 1854. He began operating a cotton gin at Lunenburg at the age of 22 and also followed the carpenter's trade for some time. In 1864 he joined the Confederate army, remaining about a year when he surrendered at Jacksonport, Arkansas.

After the close of the war he returned to Lunenburg and in 1877 engaged in the mercantile business there. In 1880 he established a business in Melbourne known by the firm name of Landers & Company. The business is still being operated, and is the oldest established mercantile business in the county. Mr. Landers was also interested in farming and livestock and had considerable real estate holdings when he died April 10, 1927.

Associated with E. G. Landers in business for many years was his son, J. HAYDEN LANDERS, who was born at Lunenburg March 12. 1881. He entered the mercantile business with his father in 1901. He operated the store until his death in November, 1946. The latter Mr. Landers was also an extensive landowner and interested in fine livestock. He was an official in the Bank of Melbourne for years, chairman of the board of deacons of the Melbourne Baptist Church for 20 years, and was a member of various boards connected with civic and agricultural improvements. His widow lives at Melbourne and his two sons, Earl Landers and Dr. Gardner Landers, live at Batesville. Dr. Landers was a colonel in the last World War.

THOMAS H. LINN was born November 2, 1867, near Mountain View, Stone County (Izard County at that time). He moved from there to near Lunenburg when about three years old. He was one of 11 children, six girls and five boys. He attended the common schools of the county until he was 18 when he taught his first school at the Rose Schoolhouse, near Melbourne, at $25 per month.

He attended the academies at Melbourne and Barren Fork. He took correspondence courses from a school in New York. In 1890 he went to Texas where he taught for five years, one year of which as principal of Bartlett High School. He then returned to Izard County where he made his home the rest of his life except one year at Desha, Independence County.

He began teaching at Melbourne in September, 1902, and continued to teach until 1912 when he went to Zion where he remained teaching until he was elected clerk of the county in 1914. He was appointed county examiner in 1904 and served four years. He was appointed again in 1911 and served three years. He was re-elected clerk in 1916.

He was elected the county's first superintendent of schools in 1918 when the officer was elected by popular vote. The superintendent was later selected by a county board of education, which re-elected him until 1926. After retiring from public office, he continued to teach until 1938, filling positions in schools at Sidney, Oxford, Mt. Olive, Guion and Melbourne.

Among other public activities, Mr. Linn served on the local draft board during World War I. He was also chairman of the Izard County Chapter of the American Red Cross for two years during the war, during which time he went before the people and made speeches in the interest of food conservation and the sale of Liberty Bonds.

He was always active in church work and worthy public causes. He reared a fine family. He died April 20, 1944. His widow lives at Melbourne.

J. O. LINN, Melbourne justice of the peace, in 1947 rounded out his 40th year in this capacity, having served in two townships continuously since 1904 except for two years when he did not allow his name to be placed on the ballot. He first served for 12 years in Sage township and when he moved to Melbourne in 1918 was elected in this township. For the past two years Mr. Linn has been serving as municipal judge of Melbourne in addition to his duties as justice of the peace. Then in June, 1947, another duty was added—he was appointed referee in chancery by Chancellor Paul Ward.

As justice of the peace he has heard over 5,000 cases, and he estimates that for every civil case heard he has settled two "out of court," effecting compromises and amicable settlements. He has also performed about 1,000 marriage ceremonies.

In addition to his judicial career, Mr. Linn (a brother of T. H. Linn, also mentioned in this volume) has taught school a third of a century and given considerable interest to farming. He said he did not get to attend school more than two months out of a year until he was 22. Now well into his seventies "Judge" Linn still hears more "court procedure" than the combined sessions of circuit, chancery and county courts at the county seat.

ROBERT G. ("BOB") MILLER, the only Izard County elective official to lose his life in World War II, was born near Zion September 3, 1910. He attended school at Zion and Sage, and finished Melbourne High School with the class of 1930. He spent some time clerking in the store of his father, G. H. Miller, at Melbourne, and worked for the State Highway Department three years under the administration of Governor Futrell. He was elected treasurer of Izard County in 1936. He was re-elected in 1938 without an opponent. In 1940 he was elected county and circuit clerk, and re-elected in 1942, making both races unopposed. He was named county chairman of the American Red Cross in 1940 and served until he entered the army March 23, 1944. He served in the infantry, 423rd Regiment, 106th Division, until December 18, 1944, when he was killed by a blast from German artillery at Radscheid, Germany.

Mr. Miller was active in civic affairs of his community and county, ever ready to lend a helping hand to any worthwhile endeavor. He was also active in Masonic work. He became a member of Little Rock 32nd Degree Consistory November 8, 1943. His widow, Mrs. Nobia Miller, and children reside at Melbourne.

THE MILLER MILITARY FAMILY. Mr. and Mrs. G. H. Miller of Melbourne held the honor of having six sons in the armed services during World War II, an honor probably equaled by few other families in the country.

Charles Miller entered the service in December, 1942.

He was a sergeant in the Radio Squadron. Thomas entered service in April, 1943. He was a corporal, and served overseas. R. G. was inducted in March, 1944. He was killed in Germany. Lowell and J. C. were inducted at the same time, April 19, 1944. Both entered the Navy. G. H. Miller, Jr., the youngest, was the last to enter service. He was barely 17 when he joined the navy in December, 1944. Also, a son-in-law, Melvin Wommack, entered service in December, 1942, and served with the medical detachment in England.

ARTHUR GRAY MASHBURN, former attorney general of Nevada, was born December 13, 1872, in Jackson County, but moved with his parents to Izard County when young. He attended the North Arkansas Academy at Old Philadelphia. He then took a business course at Nashville, Tennessee. He returned to Izard County and taught school for several years. He joined the faculty of the Arkansas School for the Deaf, Little Rock, for five years, going from there to the state of Washington where he taught in a school for the deaf for two years. He returned to Arkansas and studied law at the University of Arkansas from which he received the LL.B. degree. He then moved to Nevada and was later elected attorney general of that state. He served in this capacity 12 years, retiring to private practice about four years ago. He now lives at Carson City, Nevada.

E. E. MASHBURN, brother of Arthur Gray Mashburn, was born three miles north of Melbourne October 16, 1881. After attending the North Arkansas Academy under J. W. C. Gardner for several months, he entered the University of Arkansas from which he graduated with the degree of Bachelor of Civil Engineering in 1907. After this he surveyed railroad routes in Arkansas for about two years. He then spent two years in survey work in Brazil, South America. He went into private engineering practice in 1914 and continued until 1933 when he joined the Arkansas State Highway Department. He still works with this department and makes his home in Little Rock.

WILLIAM A. OLDFIELD was born near Franklin February 4, 1874. He attended the common schools of this county mostly at Franklin and Myron. He finished the school courses taught at Melbourne and LaCrosse, and later entered Arkansas College at Batesville. He graduated with the B. A. degree from this institution in 1896. He then took up the practice of law and was elected prosecuting attorney of the Third Judicial District in 1902 and was re-elected in 1904, serving in this capacity until October 31, 1906.

When the war broke out between the United States and Spain, in 1898, he enlisted in Company M, Second Arkansas Infantry, as a private. He was promoted to first sergeant of the same company, and later to first lieutenant. He was mustered out with that rank in March, 1899.

Mr. Oldfield represented the Second Congressional District, in which Izard County is included, from 1909 to 1928. He had some opposition, but was re-elected again and again by great majorities over his opponents.

He was elected to membership on the Ways and Means Committee in 1915, and was one of the leading Democratic members of that committee. He was selected Democratic whip at the beginning of the 67th Congress, and oldtimers of both parties testify that no more efficient whip has ever served on either side of the House. Later he was unanimously elected as chairman of the National Democratic Congressional Campaign Committee.

He had been elected to his tenth term in Congress when he died in Washington, D. C., November 19, 1928.

RICHARD H. POWELL became a resident of Izard County

in 1861. He was born in Virginia, April 18, 1827, son of Capt. Thomas Powell. In 1855 he was a student of the Cumberland Law School, graduated and was admitted to the bar the same year. He settled at Lewisburg, Tennessee, and practiced law there until 1860, when he moved to Batesville and entered into a law partnership with Elisha Baxter. The next year he moved to Izard County and settled on a farm.

In 1862 he became a member of the Legislature, but afterwards entered the Confederate army and served till the close of the war. He joined Company B, Freeman's battalion, Shaler's company, and although entering the ranks as a private, he was afterwards chosen by his company to be first lieutenant, in which capacity he served until December, 1863. He was taken prisoner near Batesville, and was sent to Little Rock. At the time he was taken prisoner he had been made commissionary and quartermaster by Gen. Price and had in his possession some valuable papers and about $1,500 in money. The United States forces secured the papers but failed to get the money. A Mrs. Montgomery managed to slip the money from the outside pocket of his overshirt, and sent it to Col. Freeman. After being sent to Little Rock, he was shortly afterwards removed to St. Louis and quartered in the McDowell College in February, 1864. The following April he was taken to Johnson's Island, and was there retained until January, 1865. Near the last of this month he was exchanged and then came home on a two months' leave of absence. He had started back to join his command when he heard of Gen. Lee's surrender.

He surrendered at Jacksonport on June 5, 1865, and returned to his home in Izard County.

After returning home he engaged in agricultural pursuits until 1866, when he again took up the practice of law in Izard and adjoining counties. In the same year he was elected judge of the Seventh Judicial Circuit, and served until after the reconstruction of 1868, when he was disfranchised. From 1868 to 1874 Judge Powell gave his attention to the mercantile business, establishing himself in LaCrosse, Lunenburg and Newburg, in Izard County, and at Paraquet Bluff, Independence County. After this Judge Powell gave four more years to the practice of law. In 1878 he was elected judge of the Third Judicial Circuit, and filled this position until 1882, when there was a division in the circuit and he was placed in charge of the Fourteenth Judicial Circuit in which capacity he served until 1890. He died at Ft. Smith April 12, 1917.

E. C. RODMAN of Calico Rock is dean of bankers in Izard County. He has been employed regularly in bank work since 1909, with the exception of two years in the army during World War I. He was cashier of the old Bluff City Bank at Calico Rock from 1912 to 1914 when the bank was consolidated with the Peoples Bank of Calico Rock to form the present State Bank of Calico Rock. He has served as cashier of the latter bank since its organization.

Mr. Rodman has missed very few state conventions of the Arkansas Bankers Association. He once served as secretary of Group Two of the association, and served three terms on the Executive Council. At present he is chairman of the North Central Clearing House of the Arkansas Bankers Association.

He was born at Pineville—and he didn't say when. He attended school at Mt. Pleasant and Calico Rock, and completed a business course. With the exception of two years residence in Oklahoma, he has made his home in Izard County. He has served on the Calico Rock school board continuously since 1926—and is still serving. He is ever interested in schools, churches and other matters of public concern.

HISTORY OF IZARD COUNTY

JAMES H. ROTEN, who for years in days gone by sponsored the annual Izard County reunion for Confederate soldiers, was born in Tennessee April 30, 1845. He came to Arkansas with his parents in 1850 and settled in Carroll County. Six years later, the family moved to Missouri. At the age of 11, he hired himself to the American Fur Company to drive a team in the wilds of the early Indian Territory (now Oklahoma) and trade with the Indians.

Mr. Roten served in the Confederate army four years during the Civil War, saw active service in 37 battles and came through without a scratch. It was during the war that he met his wife—and under peculiar circumstances. A group of 12 to 15 plunderers had gone to her mother's home to take away the only horse. Young Roten heard the woman crying. Alone he rushed up to the log cabin, commanded the release of the horse, and ordered the men to leave, which they did. Then he ate dinner with the woman and her daughter, and a mutual friendship sprang up between James Roten and the daughter, Miss Nancy Shell, which ripened into love and marriage.

They lived together 63 years before she died in 1928. They reared 10 children. He died at his home near Sage June 21, 1930. Many people still remember "Uncle Jim" Roten as the erect old man who was always on the platform dressed in his Confederate uniform at the summer reunion and picnic which was usually held at "Shell Spring," near Zion.

DR. HARLIN H. SMITH, for many years a practicing physician and surgeon at Calico Rock, was born near Calico Rock May 16, 1881. He was reared on a farm and received his early education in the rural schools of the county. He attended school for a time in the old Barren Fork Academy.

HISTORY OF IZARD COUNTY

Having chosen medicine as his profession, he read for a few months under his subsequent partner, Dr. Roe, and then attended the Medical Department of the University of Arkansas at Little Rock, from which he graduated in 1906. After this he began practicing at Calico Rock where he remained the rest of his life. In 1910 he took post-graduate work in the Kansas Post Graduate School of Medicine. Later he completed two terms in Tulane University, New Orleans, and short courses in medical colleges in Kansas City, Chicago, St. Louis and Memphis.

From 1911 until his death in 1931, he was resident surgeon of the Missouri Pacific Railroad. He was for a time secretary of the branch of the Arkansas Medical Association devoted to diseases of children. He served as Izard County coroner for several years and was on the Advisory Medical Board which served the territory of Baxter, Stone, Fulton, Independence and Izard counties during World War I.

Dr. Smith was active in fraternity organizations. He was a member of the Blue Lodge, and in 1905 he was made a Master Mason at Pineville; he received the 32nd degree in 1921 at the Albert Pike Consistory, Little Rock. He was also made a Shriner the same year by the Sahara Temple A.A.O.N.M.S. of Pine Bluff.

He was also active in civic affairs and a great booster for his town, county and state. He played an important part in making the annual Tri-County Fair at Calico Rock in the early 20's a success. He was also instrumental in bringing about a renewed interest in violin and quartette music. He sponsored several old fiddlers' contests in and out of Izard County, and was the chief factor in organizing the "Hillbilly Quartette" which achieved some fame in the early days of radio, broadcasting from KTHS, Hot Springs.

Dr. Smith died in a Little Rock hospital October 14, 1931.

A FAMILY OF DOCTORS. Mr. and Mrs. S. R. Smith, who lived at Lunenburg back in the early days, set a record for bringing into the world a family of medical doctors. Five sons, all born at Lunenburg, made M. D.'s. Two of these sons, Dr. Henry Smith of Oxford and Dr. Jeff Smith of Violet Hill, are still living and practicing medicine. Three sons, Drs. R. L., James L. and Sol W., have passed on. Dr. R. L. Smith died at Melbourne a few years ago.

Dr. James L. Smith practiced for years at Oxford. He had three sons to become doctors—Dr. J. E. Smith of Reno who is also state senator from Randolph County; Dr. Oscar Smith of Biggers, and Dr. C. Thurman Smith, who is a practicing dental surgeon in Little Rock. Dr. J. E. Smith has two sons practicing medicine. Dr. Henry Smith had one son to die while taking his pre-med course, and he has a grandson practicing medicine. Dr. Jeff Smith had a son, Dr. Cecil Smith, a dentist, who lost his life in World War I. Two daughters of Dr. R. L. Smith made graduate nurses, and a daughter of Dr. Oscar Smith is now taking her first year of medicine.

So far, the family has developed 13 doctors, two nurses and two medical students.

P. C. SHERRILL, county judge during the building of the brick courthouse in Izard County, was born near Cushman, Independence County, November 17, 1866. He grew up on a farm and attended the common school in his district. He followed farming during his early life. Later his attention was drawn to the lumber and milling business in Izard County, and he located his first sawmill near Newburg. His firm was known as Sherrill & Company, and for 10 years he did a wide range of business in that section.

He was a member of the Republican party, and, since the

county has always been strongly Democratic, he was probably the only Republican county judge in the county's history. He was nominated for the office by the county Republican convention in 1910 and in the general election defeated his Democratic opponent by a ratio of almost 16 to 1. He was re-elected in 1912. Most important of his activities while in office was the building of a new courthouse for the county.

He made the race for a third term but was narrowly defeated by his Democratic opponent, W. D. Wallace. Mr. Sherrill never again took part in political activities, but gave his time to the practice of law until his death in 1924.

MRS. NELLIE TREVATHAN, editor and writer, was born near LaCrosse in 1875 and attended the LaCrosse Collegiate Institute. Her husband, the late George H. Trevathan, was one-time editor of a paper at Melbourne. The Trevathans took over the *Batesville Guard* in 1908. When Mr. Trevathan died in 1917, Mrs. Trevathan assumed editorship of the paper and, with the assistance of her sons, Johnny, Jared and the late Allen Trevathan, published the daily paper until 1931.

Mrs. Trevathan also was well-known throughout the state as a feature writer, having contributed to the *Arkansas Gazette* and other publications. She was active in state literary circles, having served as poet laureate of the Arkansas Press Association and secretary of both the state U. D. C. and D. A. R. She also was state historian of the U. D. C. While at Batesville Mrs. Trevathan was active in civic affairs and church work, serving as chairman of the Liberty Bond drive in the Batesville district during World War I.

She died in Little Rock August 1, 1942.

Two sons, Johnny and Jared, have been active in newspaper work almost from childhood. Johnny is now a compositor on the *Arkansas Democrat*, and Jared is editor and publisher of the *Batesville News Review*.

JOHN H. WOODS, who taught the first term of school ever held in Melbourne, was born in Tennessee March 27, 1849. When he was very young, the family moved to Kentucky. When he was seven, they moved to Arkansas. He got most of his schooling in the Spring Hill district, near Oxford. At the age of 19 he entered the LaCrosse Collegiate Institute the first day of its opening. He attended school there about three years, and then taught district schools from 1870 to 1877. He was licensed to practice law in 1877. He was county examiner from 1876 to 1880. It was his duty to hold quarterly examinations, but most of them were private or individual and all oral. He held four institutes.

In the later years of his life he gave full time to the practice of law, and was considered one of the best read lawyers in this part of the state. He died March 3, 1930.

JOHN P. WOODS, practicing attorney of Fort Smith and son of the late John H. Woods of Melbourne, was born at Melbourne December 25, 1886. After finishing school at Melbourne, he entered the University of Arkansas from which he graduated in 1909 with the B. A. degree and in 1912 with the LL.B. degree. He began practicing law at Fort Smith in 1915 and has continued there since.

He served in the Arkansas Legislature from Sebastian County in 1915. At the outbreak of World War I he entered as a first lieutenant, and was later promoted to captain. The principal battles in which he fought were San Mihiel and Meuse-Argonne. He was promoted for gallantry in action September 14, 1918, and was severely wounded the following October 28. He was awarded Divisionat Citation. Purple Heart.

HISTORY OF IZARD COUNTY

Mr. Woods was presidential elector from the Fourth Congressional District in 1928. He was a member of the Fort Smith school board for 17 years, past president of Noon Civic Club, past director of both Hardscrabble Country Club and Fort Smith Chamber of Commerce, and is an active member of a number of other civic clubs. He was a member of the Arkansas Police Commission 1935-36, and has been a member of the Arkansas Bar Rules Committee since 1939. He is also chairman of the Executive Committee of the Arkansas Bar Association, and was president of the University of Arkansas Alumni Association 1938-39. He has four sons.

R. H. ("BOB") WOOD was born at Calico Rock December 28, 1913. After graduation from the Calico Rock High School he entered the University of Arkansas, from which he graduated with the LL.B. degree in 1937. He was Izard County's representative in the state Legislature the same year. He did not seek re-election, but ran for prosecuting attorney of the Sixteenth Judicial District and was elected. He served two terms in this capacity and then voluntarily retired to the practice of law at Calico Rock and Melbourne. In April, 1943, he began working in the Claim Department of the United States Fidelity and Guaranty Company in Little Rock. He was inducted into the army in March, 1944. He was discharged in June, 1946, as staff sergeant, and returned to his position with the Fidelity and Guaranty Company at the San Antonio, Texas, office where he and his family now reside.

JOHN Q. WOLF, well-known writer and former banker of Batesville, was born near Calico Rock December 13, 1864. After attending the old Spring Creek Academy, Mr. Wolf got his first job as clerk in a drug store at Calico Rock. Later he was employed as bookkeeper in the W. E. Maxfield store at that place. In 1885 he completed a business course at Bryant & Stratton's Business College in St. Louis. In 1886 he became bookkeeper for H. H. Hinkle at Melbourne. The next year he and Mr. Hinkle started a bank at Batesville in an upstairs room of the S. A. Hail book store. Hinkle & Wolf, Bankers, was the pleasing sign flung to the breeze. In 1889 the bank was organized into the Bank of Batesville. Mr. Wolf continued as cashier of the bank until it was absorbed in late years by the A. B. Banks & Company—45 years in all. He was elected president of the Arkansas Bankers convention in May, 1889.

During the past several years Mr. Wolf has spent much of his time writing feature stories for the *Arkansas Gazette* and other newspapers. Most of these stories pertain to the early history of the White River country, and his series of articles about steamboat days on White River, published in the *Gazette*, were widely acclaimed.

THOMAS H. WREN, prominent lawyer of Okemah, Oklahoma, was born near Sage March 23, 1874. He attended the district school at "Nubbin Ridge." He farmed for several years, then moved to Texas in 1895. He continued farming until 1898, and then went to Roswell, New Mexico, where he worked on a railroad and at other jobs. He entered the New Mexico Military Institute at Roswell in 1900, graduating in 1904 as second honor graduate. He was commissioned a second lieutenant in the New Mexico National Guard. He worked in Missouri and Cuba for some time, and was first assistant to the director of the Agricultural Station at Santiago de las Vegas, near Havana.

He entered the law department of the University of Michigan in 1905, graduating three years later with the LL.B. degree. After locating in Oklahoma, he has been assistant county attorney, city attorney, county judge, and representative in the Oklahoma Legislature. He served in the Oklahoma cavalry, advancing from sergeant to captain. He has served as conciliation commissioner for Okfuskee County, Oklahoma, since 1934.

Since establishing permanent residence at Okemah, he has served in many and varied capacities of public activities in his town and county. He has also had no small part in important state activities. He has taught many years in the Bible School of the church of Christ, of which he is a member. He is a brother of P. O. Wren of LaCrosse.

BRIEFS OF OTHERS

To give biographical sketches of all the natives of Izard County who have attained distinction in other towns, counties and states would be all but an endless task. Due to lack of space and information only honorable mention can be given to many:

L. C. Gulley, born and reared in Izard County, was onetime superintendent of Schofield Barracks in Honolulu, and when he died in California recently, left one of the largest collections of relics and antiques in the country. His brother, Wilbur Gulley, is a prominent loan agent in Little Rock.

The late E. E. Godwin was a former assistant attorney general of Arkansas and one of the outstanding lawyers of the state. He practiced at Camden for years.

Dr. L. T. Evans of Batesville is present president of the Arkansas Medical Association and one of the leading physicians of north Arkansas. He was born at Mt. Pleasant.

Dr. John Knox Freeman, another Izardite, has been medical director of Webb Brothers School at Bell Buckle, Tennessee, for 30 years. He is the grandfather of Claude Jarman who has reached fame in moving pictures as Jody in "The

Yearling," and recently won the Junior Oscar in the movies.

C. O. Bradshaw, brother of De E. Bradshaw, became U. S. narcotic agent for the New England states. His son, Yancey Bradshaw, is now the associate producer of "March of Time."

Fred Watkins, formerly of LaCrosse, and Boyce Stubblefield, formerly of Oxford, are now among the best lawyers practicing in Little Rock.

H. F. Croom, born at Oxford, was the first president of what is now Harding College of Searcy, when the institution was located at Morrilton. He is now with a large insurance agency in Oklahoma.

Lee Rector, Th. D., was dean of Oklahoma Baptist University, Shawnee, Oklahoma, for several years, and is now a Baptist preacher in Oklahoma. He was born near Melbourne.

Van Johnson, son of the late D. O. Johnson, former Izard County sheriff, is now a practicing attorney at Texarkana. He is also court stenographer and president of the State Association of Court Stenographers.

J. T. Cone of Searcy is one of the state's leading building contractors, having constructed some of the finest church houses and other buildings in the state. He is a' native of Newburg.

Ewell Richardson is an attorney for the Federal Bureau of Investigation in Washington, D. C. He is a son of Mr. and Mrs. I. B. Richardson of Melbourne.

Dr. Otis McMurtrey, born in Izard County, is one of the leading chiropractors in California, is a member of the board of trustees of a chiropractor college and has held other prominent positions in connection with his profession.

Dr. W. D. Hinson, optometrist for Gus Blass Company

of Little Rock, was born near Violet Hill. He practiced for years at Newport.

Dr. C. E. Spann of Altheimer, Dr. Paul Jeffery of Bethesda, Dr. Arthur Billingsley of England, Dr. Charles Billingsley of Ash Flat and Dr. J. L. Weathers and Dr. O. S. Woods of Salem are Izard County natives.

Drs. Myrlas Matthews and James Milburn, both born at Calico Rock, are practicing dentists at Batesville. Dr. C. G. Hinkle of Batesville is also a native of Izard County.

Earl R. Wiseman, who practiced law for years at Calico Rock, was state revenue commissioner for four years, and is now with the Internal Revenue Department in Oklahoma City.

Among Izardites who have made leaders in the business world in towns outside the county must be mentioned Hanley Powell of Batesville; Vernon Powell of Beebe; W. E. Baxter of England; Austin (deceased) and Roscoe Billingsley of Wayne, Oklahoma; Ewell Billingsley of Newport; Frank Carder of Searcy; Paul Morgan of Mountain Home; Sam Rector of Heber Springs; Paul Meers of Little Rock; D. E. and Ray McSpadden of North Little Rock; Coy Wilson of Little Rock; J. W. Williamson (deceased) of Batesville; W. T. McJunkins (deceased) of Ash Flat; Troy Gaston of Oklahoma City; Clyde Crutchfield of Dallas, Texas; Kelsie Halbrook of Wayne, Oklahoma; H. H. Harris of Corning; E. R. Hall of Memphis, Tennessee; Earl Landers of Batesville; V. H. Ragan of Little Rock; Davis Hill of Rector, and L. U. Crutchfield of Sulphur, Oklahoma.

Freas Crutchfield, born near Zion, is postmaster of Batesville.

Judge A. H. Benbrook of Fairfield, Texas, was born near

Wideman. He has been a county judge in Texas for about 20 years, never having been defeated for the office.

Brooke Wallace, postmaster at Wayne, Oklahoma, for the past 15 years, was born near LaCrosse.

Dr. James Dillard and Dr. Harber, both natives of Izard County, are prominent physicians in Oklahoma, both operating hospitals in that state.

Roy N. Jeffery, native of Mt. Olive, established the Roy N. Jeffery Lumber Company at Batesville, one of the largest lumber and building material concerns in the state.

Dr. Tasso Edwards, born at Mt. Pleasant, has been practicing dentistry at Bald Knob for many years.

John W. Taylor, native of Izard County, is now justice of the peace of Uvalde, Texas, home of former Vice-President John Nance Garner. Mr. Taylor taught singing schools in Izard County for a number of years.

www.ingramcontent.com/pod-product-compliance
Lightning Source LLC
Chambersburg PA
CBHW071430160426
43195CB00013B/1858